NO PLACE BUT HOME

Reflections on Meditation and the Spiritual Life

NO PLACE BUT HOME:

Reflections on Meditation and the Spiritual Life

By Jeff Carreira

Copyright © 2019

Emergence Education & Jeff Carreira

ISBN-10: 0-9995658-4-2

ISBN-13: 978-0-9995658-4-1

Emergence Education Press

P.O. Box 63767, Philadelphia, PA 19147

www.EmergenceEducation.com

Cover design by Silvia Rodrigues

NO PLACE BUT HOME

Reflections on Meditation and the Spiritual Life

JEFF CARREIRA

ACKNOWLEDGEMENTS

I dedicate this book to all of the people who travel with me on this journey of discovery - your sincerity and commitment is a constant and invaluable source of inspiration to me.

It is also dedicated to those many extraordinary individuals from whom I have learned so much. Some are still alive and still teaching me, others are long since passed, but their wisdom lives on in the great works they have left behind.

I owe special thanks to Ariela Cohen who worked tremendously hard compiling, sorting and editing through the raw material for this book. Thank you, this would not have happened without your efforts.

And once again, thank you Jill Ouellette for your careful eye in proofreading the final manuscript.

CONTENTS

The soul should always stand ajar, ready to welcome the ecstatic experience.
— Emily Dickinson

Close your eyes and surrender. — Rumi

There is always more mystery. — Anaïs Nin

The key to growth is the introduction of higher dimensions of consciousness into our awareness. — Lao Tzu

All that is required to realize the Self is to be still. — Ramana Maharshi

I myself, am the center that exists only because the geometry of the abyss demands it.
— Fernando Pessoa

Mysticism is the art of union with Reality. — Evelyn Underhill

I believe that much unseen is also here. — Walt Whitman

INTRODUCTION

This is a book about life or, more specifically, about living fully. It's an exploration about what it means to be awake to who you really are and what you are truly capable of. It's about opening to the full potential of being human.

The central question we will explore in these pages asks us to consider what it is that lives our lives. We will be tempted to simply rattle off, "Me, I live my life." That answer seems too obvious to question, but those things that seem too obvious to question are often the things we need to question most.

Who or what is living your life right now?

The underlying assumption of this book is that the energy of life - the wisdom, compassion and intelligence that moves through us - is not a personal possession. It originates in each one of us from the same universal source.

We did not appear as a living thing in a dead and unconscious universe. This is a living, conscious universe and the life and consciousness that we appear to possess is ultimately sourced from the whole.

This universal living consciousness is the spirit that animates us. When we perceive, it perceives. When we feel, it feels through us. When we act, it is that which moves us.

We are being lived by a universal source of energy, wisdom and love, but that mysterious force does not emerge through us without distortion. Our fears cause contractions that cut off the flow. Our desires bend that energy to suit our will. Our beliefs and assumptions shape our world.

This is a spiritual book. It's about becoming a more open vessel for the universal flow of life, love and wisdom. As we already said, this book is about living fully, awakening to who you really are, and discovering the full potential of being human. You are a cosmic being longing to express your full potential.

The first thing we need to realize is that the energy and intelligence pouring through us is caught up in our preoccupations. It is being filtered through our fears and concerns, our desires and aspirations, and our ideas and beliefs.

The first step in the journey is to liberate ourselves from habits of mental reactivity. We relentlessly react to whatever our minds present to us. We push things away and pull others closer. We ignore some aspects of our experience and obsess over the rest.

We are caught in loops of habitual ways of feeling, thinking, perceiving, and behaving. These patterns limit our lives and, unless we free ourselves from them, the energy that animates us can only express itself in predictable ways. In this book, you will be guided in a form of meditation that allows you to free yourself from your familiar and limiting mental tendencies.

Our tendencies don't necessarily have to go away; we just need to learn how to step out of them. Through diligent practice, you will discover how to simply step out of your mind, allow it to do whatever it wants, without any of it bothering you in the least.

This immaculate freedom of mind is the first step of the journey. The second step involves the expansion of our perception. Once our awareness has been liberated from the relentless mental loops and conditioned patterns of mind, something miraculous happens. We see beyond the mind.

We realize that our awareness had been fixated on a tiny area of consciousness, and that left us all but blind to the vast expanse of consciousness beyond. Having freed ourselves from the prison of the familiar, we are available to see and be moved by dimensions of reality that were too subtle for us to notice before.

As this book deepens, you will enter a second journey of awakening that involves aligning with deeper aspects of who we are and allowing ourselves to be carried off into a new life.

The goal of this book is to liberate the living conscious energy of this universe in you so it can carry you to ever higher human potentials.

Welcome to the adventure.

PART ONE
FOUNDATIONS OF THE SPIRITUAL JOURNEY

In this part of the book, we explore the philosophical underpinnings and inquiries that will create the most fertile inner space for our awakening experience to take root in.

CHAPTER ONE
A RETURN TO INNOCENCE

In this book you will discover a form of meditation that acts as a leverage point to catapult you into a different reality. In order to open ourselves up to the profound spiritual transformation that meditation makes possible, we must first realize that our perception of reality is made up of a hopeless tangle of sensation and interpretation.

In other words, what we assume to be reality as we look out at the world is not objectively real in the way we've been taught. It is a perception of reality interpreted through a lens of ideas and attitudes that we have acquired through our personal experience and inherited from the culture we live in. And, to a large extent, we are blind to the ideas and attitudes that are shaping our experience of reality.

The journey of spiritual transformation can be seen as an escape from our current set of assumptions about reality. As we will see in this book, the practice of meditation is an invaluable aid to spiritual transformation because it allows us to relax our habits of interpretation so we can see beyond them.

If our interest in meditation is fueled by a desire to transform at the deepest levels of our being, then it is essential that we deconstruct some of our assumptions about what is real before we begin to explore the practice. Otherwise our meditation practice will remain embedded in the very same set of assumptions that we want to be liberated from.

One way to begin the process of deconstruction is to realize that almost all of us believe in an outdated myth. This myth is the unconscious belief that we are standing on some solid ground of truth from which the rest of our understanding is built. This belief gives us confidence in what we think is true, because we assume that underneath our ideas about reality there is something authentically real.

Look around you right now. Don't you assume that you are looking at reality? You assume that the things you see are actually real things. In fact, the reality of what you see is what differentiates reality from dreams. In a dream, we see things that we think are real but, when we wake up, we realize that none of it actually was. The dream was an illusion of reality created by our minds.

Spiritual transformation is often compared to waking up from a dream in the sense that when you wake up spiritually you realize that so much of what you thought was real never was. So much of reality was simply constructed by the filtering and interpreting habits of our minds.

In order to pursue meditation, to the depths of awareness that will allow us to see the illusion of the only reality we have ever known, requires a profound commitment and penetrating clarity of intention. In order to cultivate the depth commitment and clarity of intention necessary, we must first know beyond any doubt that we are not seeing reality as it is.

We constantly assume that the way we see reality is the way that reality actually is. Generally, it is only after the fact, when we realize that we have made a mistake, that we recognize that what we had thought was real was not. The path of transformation invites us to go so far down the road of uncertainty that we start to doubt all of our beliefs, as opposed to concluding that there is no reality, because that would of course be another belief about reality. We just need to realize that we don't know what is real. Then we're free to discover radically new ways of seeing.

It is important to realize that our perception of reality is made up of interpretations, assumptions and conclusions built layer upon layer. The concepts we are currently aware of sit on a mountain of earlier assumptions that have built up over time. The earliest beliefs about reality were laid down long ago and, based on those, new layers of understanding were built. Each new layer of concepts becomes the assumptions that the next layers of understanding are built on. And so on and so on and so on.

Look out at the world. What do you see? What do you really see? You might think you are looking at chairs, and books, and tables, and carpets, but are you really? What do you really see? Isn't it all just shapes and colors? Isn't everything else an interpretation?

The experience you are having right now as you look at this book, or scan the room in front of you, is, as the philosopher William James put it, thick with interpretation. You think you are looking at a room, but there is no such thing as a room. A room is an idea, a concept. We think it is a real thing because we are trained to interpret our experience in terms of concepts. We live in a conceptualized world.

As we get started on our mystical journey, it is crucial that we see the difference between sensation and perception. We are trained to filter and interpret our sensations to form meaningful perceptions of the world. We take the shapes and colors in front of us and turn them into chairs and tables and books and everything else.

If we start to sift through all of the assumptions that lie hidden within our current perception of reality, we will find a primary assumption about ourselves lying beneath them all. No matter what you see, hear, taste, feel, or think in any way, underneath it all is a sense of being the one who is seeing, hearing, tasting, feeling or thinking. The assumption that we exist as a separate self is embedded in every single experience we have.

The path of deep meditation can take us so far that we can even begin to question our own existence and this is of supreme importance because the goal of mysticism is the recognition of Oneness. The discovery that there is no separation and that all of existence is one indivisible wholeness.

If this is the ultimate goal we seek, then the primary obstacle to spiritual transformation is the assumption that, when we look out at the world, we are looking at something real that exists separate from us. Why? because the belief that I am an independent entity looking out at a world that stands apart from me is the very source of the illusion of separation that we want to be free from.

The reason we have to find a way to authentically question all of our beliefs and assumptions about reality is because the doorway to transformation is profound innocence.

What happens when you see something that you've never seen before? You don't have any conception about what it is so you look more deeply. You see more fully what is there.

When we talk about meditation we often talk about beginner's mind. On the one hand, this means always being a beginner in meditation so you never get comfortable in the practice and your senses remain alert. At a deeper level, it means becoming innocent about life so that we can see everything including ourselves as if for the first time.

The whole point here is to say it is natural that we will want to approach our meditation practice using the same tools of perception and rationality that have served us so well in other parts of our lives, but those tools will not serve us in the quest for spiritual transformation.

The shift in awareness that meditation offers is so deep and foundational that it can only be experienced wholesale. It is an instantaneous flip into a new way of seeing. You can't work into it step by step. You can't figure it out. It just happens. And the practice of meditation makes it more likely that it will.

CHAPTER TWO
INTUITION AND UNDERSTANDING

There is a very important distinction that we need to make between two different kinds of knowing – experience and understanding.

Experience is the knowing of things directly. This type of knowing appears to our senses simply by virtue of what is there without us doing anything at all. It is immediately present to awareness and because it is immediate it cannot be denied. For instance, I can see a ghost in the attic and doubt that it was a ghost – but I cannot reasonably deny that I saw something. We can only deny our understanding about our experience, not the fact of having it.

Understanding is the knowing about things. It comes to us in the form of the inner language of thought. Did you ever go to sleep someplace other than your own bed and then wake up and not immediately remember where you are? For a few seconds, you are disoriented. You are experiencing the room around you, but you do not have access to any understanding about the room. Inevitably, you remember that you are in Aunt Jo's guest room. Suddenly, your mental picture fills out with an understanding about where you are and, suddenly, you know a great deal about the room. You know that you are spending a weekend with your family. You remember that down the hall there is a staircase that will take you to the main floor of the house and that your brother is sleeping in a room across the hall. Your experience 'of' the room is filled out with your understanding 'about' the room.

In the philosophy of American Transcendentalist Ralph Waldo Emerson, the knowing of experience was called reason and so the distinction we are talking about was known as the distinction between reason and understanding.

The notion of reason was thought of as an intuitive knowing. It was the self evident knowing that isn't derived from rational deduction but, instead, is the knowing that comes from directly perceived pure awareness.

Understanding, on the other hand, is the knowing-about-things that is contained in explanations, interpretations and logic.

The distinction between reason and understanding was originally articulated by Samuel Taylor Coleridge in a book entitled *Aides to Reflection*. According to Coleridge, reason is a direct product of the reasoning faculty. It is an "accident" of reason. His use of the word accident is not typical these days. What he means by describing reason as accidental is that it appears spontaneously without warning or precursor. Reason is spontaneous knowing. It is not an understanding that is constructed through any thought process. It is the direct and self-authenticating recognition of truth. The other element implied in the word accident is that it is unavoidable. The direct knowing of truth happens spontaneously and also compulsively. The reasoning faculty is 'knowing' itself. It is not a process that leads to knowing. This implies that there is some part of us that simply knows the truth and cannot help but know it.

Understanding for Coleridge is "an abstraction which the human mind forms by reflecting on its own thoughts and forms of thinking." This knowing is a natural product of the process of mind and it is bound up in, and limited by, language. He also asserted that it is a process that requires no "self" to enact. It is a natural process of the lawful interaction of mental elements, a simple unfolding of the characteristics of the mind in nature.

We could say that some things in reality force themselves upon us immediately. They appear spontaneously without provocation and they impress themselves upon our senses in ways that we cannot avoid. These things surely must be real. Direct sense impressions – smells, tastes, sensations, sounds and sights – simply appear in awareness. We don't call them into being and we cannot alter or avoid the way they present themselves. Ideas and intuitions also, upon their initial appearance, share the same unalterable immediacy of presence.

The world presents itself to us through a series of spontaneous, immediate and unalterable first impressions. At its core, before we can do anything about it, our experience emerges as an unending parade of first impressions – a relentless succession of pure experiences. Only after the reality of the world presents itself in this way can our minds then go

to work constructing an understanding about the world that presents itself.

In summary, reason is the knowing of experience - the knowing-of-things that appears to our senses simply as what is there without us doing anything. It is immediately and directly present to awareness with no intermediate activity on our part. Because it is immediate, it cannot be denied. On the other hand, understanding is the knowing-about-things that is derived through the inner language of thought.

We could extend the idea of reason to include intuitions of all kinds. Intuition, we could say, is the experience of pure knowing. It is a kind of knowing that verifies itself by the virtue of its immediacy. Intuitions appear spontaneously and avoidably like an accident. We all experience intuitions. Sometimes you just know something because you know it, because you feel it with a certain kind of certainty that you don't feel the need to question.

Modern culture tends to trust understanding over intuition. We are taught to trust ideas based on the strength of the logic from which they were derived. In spiritual circles, on the other hand, we often find a preference for intuition in which our trust in an idea comes from the force with which it presented itself spontaneously out of nowhere.

Logic and rationality are important in our quest for spiritual transformation, but the understanding derived from logic and rationality will never be enough to fully grasp the subtle realities that the spiritual path inevitably reveals to us. Sooner or later, you will come to a point where you will need to decide to trust your spiritual intuitions or not.

CHAPTER THREE
LIVING MATTER OR SPIRIT INCARNATE

Idealism describes any philosophy in which it is assumed that mind is more foundational than matter. Any idealistic philosophy will assume that first there was mind – some form of absolute intelligence or pure consciousness. From this mind the world, the universe and all forms of living beings would come.

The main competitor of Idealism today is Materialism. In any materialistic philosophy it would be assumed that first there was an unconscious universe of matter and energy. Then, some form of matter came to life and developed consciousness.

In short, Idealists believe that some form of mind or consciousness is primary in the universe and all of the material and sensual elements of reality arise in the mind. Materialists lean in the opposite direction. They see matter as the primary reality of the universe and mind as an outgrowth of material interactions.

Having a mind and a body are two of the most fundamental experiences of being human and one of the most confounding philosophical questions involves understanding who we really are.

Are we intelligent matter – stuff that got smart – or are we incarnate spirit – smarts that grew stuff around it?

This question is inherent in the very nature of our experience of being human. We have bodies and we have the experience of consciousness – mind and matter, body and soul. Which one is more us, which came first, and which is really running the show?

The world's great religious traditions tend towards the outlook that we are spiritual beings who became flesh. First there was God, pure spirit and from God came us. Our more recent scientific understanding of reality has led many of us to believe that we were matter first that then evolved into life and intelligence. This is one of the divides that creates a rift that separates science from religion and idealists from materialists.

If we are spirit that has taken form, it means that we are sourced from beyond the physical universe. Our intelligence and will comes from a place that is free from the rest of nature. We act in nature while maintaining a foothold in some transcendent realm of spirit. Our being stands apart from and above the laws of nature and we are uniquely autonomous and responsible for our own actions in the universe.

If we are matter that interacts in ways that are complex enough to exhibit intelligence, then we are governed by the same natural laws that preside over the rest of the universe. Our thoughts and actions are simply the necessary consequence of cause and effect, in the same way that the movement of a tree blowing is a consequence of the wind. This would mean that our concept of ourselves as autonomous, willful and responsible beings would need to be re-examined.

My experiences of meditation, as you will see in this book, have led me to believe that our awareness and everything else in this universe arise from some form of absolute intelligence or pure consciousness. Meditation will not necessarily make you an Idealist, but it will challenge any of your materialistic assumptions.

It can feel strange for us to question the materialistic assumptions of our culture and entertain the possibility that this is an idealistic reality. It would mean that everything comes from some form of pure knowing. This pure knowing would not take up any space, it would not exist anywhere in space, it would have existed before time and space. This all pervasive and eternal source of awareness is what, in theistic terms, would be called God.

We have been raised in a deeply materialistic culture and we've been taught that we are fundamentally material stuff that got smart somehow. This view will be challenged as you enter the profound depths of meditation because the act of meditation involves turning your attention in on itself and, when you focus on the source of your own awareness, you will inevitably wonder where it is coming from. Is it emerging out of your brain? Or was it there before your body appeared?

CHAPTER FOUR
THE PATH OF MYSTICAL EXPERIENCE

A mystic is one who sees the deeper reality that lies hidden beneath our ordinary experience of reality. The mystic looks deeply into the nature of things by letting go of conventional wisdom and allowing their awareness to roam beyond the safety of the familiar. The mystic has tasted something that lies under the surface of things and the ordinary forms of reality alone are no longer satisfying.

According to the tradition of Western philosophy, we never experience reality as it is. Instead, we experience reality as it comes to us filtered through the mind and shaped into an intelligible form. As it passes through the mechanisms of understanding, reality becomes known to us. Our experience gets interpreted and filtered until it becomes the phenomenal world of perception, and this is the only world we can ever know. Any deeper reality from which the phenomenal world is built will remain forever unseen and invisible to us.

The mystic believes differently. The mystic is captivated by the eternal quest to see that which cannot be seen and asserts that it *is* possible to see beyond the edges of the known, if we allow ourselves to enter into the treacherous waters of radical uncertainty. *The Cloud of Unknowing* is a classic text of medieval Christian Mysticism. It teaches us the art of forgetting what is known so that we can surrender to deeper mystical truths.

William James, in *The Varieties of Religious Experience*, identified four characteristics that all mystical experiences share – ineffability, a noetic quality, transience and passivity. Mystical experiences are ineffable because they defy description. Those that have them find themselves at a loss to adequately describe their experience to others. They have a noetic quality that means that, although they cannot be described or understood, there is still an intuited knowing inherent in them. They are transient because they are fleeting in nature, arriving unexpectedly and departing in their own time. And there is a passive quality to mystical experiences in that they only show themselves in the face of surrender. You cannot will a mystical experience into being. You may do a great amount of practice and study to coax them out, but in the end, you must allow them to come into being, not force them to.

Mysticism focuses on the direct knowing of inner truths that are hidden and ordinarily remain unseen. These inner truths contain a form of wisdom about the nature of reality that can only be obtained as inner revelation. The mystic looks inward and discovers in the intuitions of the spirit deep wisdom about reality.

The mystic knows that the key to entering the realms of inner revelation is the ability to let go of the familiar. Our ordinary and familiar perceptions of reality are exactly what we must learn to see beyond if we are to taste the miraculous. To do this, we must discover how to consciously not know.

The habit of knowing in us is so strong. We compulsively feel the need to know everything. When confronted with even a small amount of uncertainty, we tend to become uneasy and immediately scramble to know again. The experience of knowing is a relief from the discomfort of uncertainty. When we find ourselves not-knowing we might often begin to rapidly sift through ideas until we find thoughts in our heads that explain reality to us. When we find an adequate explanation, the feeling of uncertainty disappears and we relax.

If we look more closely at the experience of not-knowing, we will see that there is more than just the uncomfortable tension of uncertainty. When we do-not-know, we are receptive and awake. Because we do-not-know we are looking, our senses are wide open, and we find ourselves feeling into reality in search of wisdom. This open and receptive stance is exactly the stance that the mystic is able to consciously adopt in relationship to the possibility of the miraculous.

When we know, we feel secure because we know where the edges are. We know what is true and what is not true. We know what is possible and what is not possible. Knowing surrounds us with a protective boundary that makes us feel safe from the unexpected.

If we are pursuing the mystical and the miraculous, this boundary on what is possible is exactly what we want to remove. We are actively searching for something unexpected!

We want something new and unpredictable to occur because nothing less could ever be miraculous. We must come to a place where we simply don't know what is possible.

I remember a very profound moment in my life when I was outside looking up at a beautiful blue sky and I just realized that I actually didn't know what was possible. In that moment, I could see that my ordinary experience of reality was surrounded by a sense of limitation – an unspoken invisible assumption that some things were possible and others were not and that I knew the difference between the two.

When the assumption of limitation fell away, I was overcome by a sense of awe and wonder because realizing that you didn't know what's possible is essentially the same as knowing that anything is possible.

When you slip into a state of suspended limitation you feel dizzy with possibility. You see that the ideas of what is and what is not possible have always been only ideas and were never necessarily the limits of reality. You realize that it is you who holds on to these limiting ideas and it is you that can let them go.

The Dark night of the Soul

John of the Cross was the sixteenth century Spanish monk who conceived of 'the dark night of the soul' to describe the three-part journey that must be taken to attain divine union with God.

The first part of the dark night is that time when the light of day is fading and evening is bringing on the darkness. This represents the loss of our attachment to the life that we were living. As our hearts are pulled toward holy union we move into the mysterious darkness and leave the sensual world behind. At this point, the light that brightened our previous life fades like the light of day and we are directed forward more by pushing away from what we had previously known than by any vision of where we are going.

The second part of the dark night occurs when the light of day has disappeared completely and the new dawn is far from arrival. We see nothing. Our old world is gone and yet nothing new has emerged to replace it. We are blind; and the only way to proceed is through a blind trust in the passion of our spiritual heart.

In the third part of the dark night, the new day is beginning to dawn. The light of the sacred begins to reveal itself before us. This light is not the light of our previous life because it is not a light that we see with our eyes. It is the light of divinity that can only be seen with our emerging capacities for spiritual perception. We are still blind, but we have begun to develop the ability to see anyway.

As we transform from the person we are now to who we will be tomorrow, we must travel through some version of this dark night of unknowing. No transformation can occur that does not involve disillusion.

We can grow without passing through the darkness of not knowing. We can develop. We can get stronger, smarter, and more compassionate and never have to leave the light of day. But if we want to transform, if we want to move in some fundamental way from the person we are now to the person we will become, then we must let go of who we are and we must pass through the blindness of not knowing. It takes tremendous strength and courage to transform. To deeply let go of who we are so that we can open up to the unlimited possibilities of being different.

As you continue on reading, the remainder of the reflections of this book keep these opening chapters in mind. This could easily become a book of ideas that lead to no transformation at all, but if you enter them with a heart and mind wide open to possibility, these pages have the power to catalyze a miracle in you.

PART TWO
GUIDANCE FOR MEDITATION

In this part of the book, we explore a deceptively simple approach to meditation with a degree of subtlety that will allow you to experience profound shifts in awareness.

CHAPTER FIVE
MEDITATION FOR
TRANSFORMATION

I've dedicated my life to the exploration of the profound potential for transformation that all human beings possess. In this pursuit, I've had the grace of experiencing transformation at the core of my being and I've always had other pioneering souls to share and explore with. All of that experience has brought with it an unshakeable conviction about the profound relationship between meditation and transformation. Here you will find my understanding of how and why the experience of meditation so profoundly enhances our capacity to transform.

Let me be clear that, when I talk about meditation, I'm not referring only to sitting with your eyes closed. I'm talking about deep abidance in the experience of who we are beyond the mind. The posture or form of meditation doesn't really matter. All that matters is that we move beyond our assumptions of limitation and into the wider expanse of who we are.

Our minds have been profoundly conditioned to remain relentlessly fixated on a certain range of thoughts, feelings, and sensory perceptions that actually lie within a much larger field of awareness. Because this range is what we are habituated to perceive, we assume that there is nothing else to be aware of. One of the miracles of meditation is the discovery that we can perceive more than we think we can. In fact, we are already conscious of more than we think we are.

True meditation, in the way we are speaking about it in this book, occurs when we discover how to remove our attention from anything in particular and allow it to float freely in consciousness.

When meditation occurs, it is like realizing that you can fly. You live your whole life anchored to a narrow range of thoughts, feelings and sensations, and suddenly you find yourself floating in midair. Nothing is more exhilarating or mind altering than the freedom you find in true meditation.

To understand the relationship between meditation and transformation, the first thing we have to realize is that the entirety of our current experience of being human has been carved out of a vast field of possibility.

We know that our eyes only perceive a narrow part of the electromagnetic spectrum, and our ears only hear a small range of sound frequencies. In the same way, our conditioned minds only experience a small part of the immensity of consciousness.

As I already stated, one of the great miracles that can be discovered through meditation is that we have the ability to experience consciousness beyond what we believe our minds are capable of experiencing. Our ability to experience is not limited by the conditioning of our minds. This discovery is like seeing beyond what the eye can see, or hearing more than what the ear can hear. We have much more access to consciousness than our minds are currently aware of.

The next thing that we have to realize, in order to fully appreciate the relationship between meditation and transformation, is that all of reality is in constant flux. We are born into an unintelligible rush of experience.

Slowly, we learn how to filter our perception so that we stabilize in a particular experience of being someone. Within an unceasing flow of experience, we have temporarily stabilized in the experience of being 'me.' By ceaselessly focusing on a very limited part of the ever-shifting field of experience, we learn to experience ourselves as an identifiable entity.

In order to stabilize into a particular identity, we had to practice remaining doggedly fixated on the narrow band of consciousness that creates the experience of being 'me.' That habit of riveting our attention on the experience of being me is so strong that we have forgotten that there is any other possibility. Most people live their entire lives busy being whoever they learned to be in the first place.

When we become interested in spiritual transformation, it is because we have begun, for some reason or other, to feel stifled by the fixed sense of self that we are. We start to realize that we are more than that, but we don't know how to break the habit of mental fixation that holds our current identity in place.

If we want to transform, if we want to expand our experience of consciousness and identity, we have to first unglue our attention from the small band of possibility that we have become habitually adhered to. Meditation is a practice for releasing our awareness.

The experience of freedom is the first miracle of meditation. The second is the discovery that once our attention has been liberated from strict adherence to our current sense of self, we are available to enter into a natural process of spiritual growth and mystical adventure.

Once we discover the miracle of free-floating consciousness, we begin to realize something even more miraculous. What we discover is that consciousness naturally expands as soon as we stop holding ourselves in place.

Suddenly it all makes sense. Growth is a natural part of life. Everything grows and often without much force or effort. Trees don't have to force themselves to grow from seed to maturity, nor do flowers or animals or birds. Growth is the essence of being alive.

Why wouldn't consciousness grow in the same way?

As we enter into a more natural process of spiritual growth, we realize that we have been holding on to who we are at the very same time that we have been trying to change. Pushing off of the past is just another way of holding on to it. The experience of meditation is the experience of letting go of who we are. And as soon as we let go of who we are, we enter a natural process of growth and evolution.

Deep meditation allows us to let go of all of the ways we have learned to habitually think of ourselves so that we are free to become more than that. That is why I see it as an essential part of the transformative process.

CHAPTER SIX
THE PRACTICE OF NO PROBLEM

The meditation practice that I teach is the simplest thing you can possibly do. In fact, it is so simple that you are already doing it right now without realizing it. You've been doing it for as long as you've been alive and you will continue doing it until the day you die. To be totally honest, I believe you were doing it before you were born, and will continue after you die, but we will get to all that in due time.

You can't do this meditation wrong. You literally can't miss. That is why I sometimes describe it as a magic archery range.

A magic archery range has no targets. You just shoot an arrow in any direction and wherever you aim a target appears and you hit a bull's eye...every time. You can't miss! That's the magic.

What we quickly discover in the magic archery range, is how difficult it can be to always win. That's because our minds are problem-solving machines, and they create problems out of anything – even not being able to lose.

As you approach this practice of meditation, you first have to consider if you really want to live a life where you can't miss. Are you truly ready to be content? Are you ready to give up the luxury of having a problem to escape into?

It's an important contemplation because until you're ready to have no problem you will continue to make problems for yourself. As soon as you're ready to have no problem, you will discover a new world to live in.

The basic instruction of this form of meditation is simply to have no problem. You sit still, upright and alert, and no matter what you experience, you don't make a problem out of it. There is nothing else to it.

No matter what you experience, you just don't make a problem out of it. Even if your mind tells you that you have a problem, you don't make a problem out of that either. If you really feel like something is wrong, you don't make a problem out of that. If everything in you is insisting that something is wrong, you don't have a problem with that either.

It is a tremendously easy meditation to do for a short amount of time. When the time gets longer, we find out how hard it can be to have no problem.

You can try it right now. Time yourself for five seconds while you sit still and practice having no problem.

Having no problem is easy for five seconds because your mind doesn't have enough time to even start looking for a problem. As you extend the time, it gets more difficult.

If you are vigilant with the practice eventually you will make a miraculous discovery – you don't have to have a problem even if your mind thinks you do. When you realize this, you will discover a depth of freedom from self-concern that is nearly unheard of in the world.

One typical problem our minds will fixate on in meditation is that we don't know what to focus on. "How do I do this? What do I focus on?" your mind will ask.

If you meditate long enough, you will eventually notice that no matter what problem your mind creates, it always comes in the form of an argument that's trying to convince you that something is wrong. In this case it might go like this: "What am I supposed to focus on? He didn't tell me what to focus on. I don't know what to focus on. This is not fair. It won't work. I can't do this. It can't be done because there is nothing to focus on."

You see, there is no real problem. There is just a conversation happening in your mind. And that conversation, no matter what form it takes, does not have to be a problem. It is just a conversation about a problem. If you ignore it, there is no problem to be found.

Have you ever had a friend that complains all the time? No matter what happens, they always seem to find a problem to complain about. For a while, you might talk to them about their problems. But eventually it gets exhausting. After a while you don't want to be involved with their problems. Your mind is a little like that friend. It always has a problem, and after a while it gets exhausting.

Of course, sometimes your mind is your best friend. We all want to use our mind for the things it does best, but we don't want to get involved with all of its problems – especially in meditation when objectively speaking not much can actually go wrong. After all you are just sitting still.

With your friend there are times when you just decide not to listen to them. They may even keep talking to you. But you're not really listening anymore. The same thing can happen with your mind. It'll keep complaining, "I don't know what to focus on. I don't know what to focus on. I don't know what to focus on." And you just sit there.

It's like a radio playing in the next room. You hear the sound, but you're not listening.

Every problem you will ever have in meditation will always be a conversation that your mind is having with you. All you have to do is not listen to it, and then you're free. Eventually, your mind might get bored and stops talking to you. That can be wonderful, but it doesn't matter. The point is that we don't have to wait for our mind to stop talking before we stop listening.

We might assume that once we decide to have no relationship to our thoughts and problems, they will stop, but they don't. Imagine driving a car down the highway with your foot on the gas. You may decide to take your foot off the gas, but that doesn't mean the car will stop. The car has built up a lot of momentum so it keeps going maybe for a long time. Your mind does the same thing. You may decide to stop paying attention to it, but that doesn't make it stop.

It takes time for your mind to stop because it has a lot of momentum behind it. But that's not a problem. You just let it go. It will coast to a stop eventually, and if it doesn't, who cares? It isn't hurting anything. It isn't doing anything. It can't touch you. You're free already anyway.

One of the tricky things about The Practice of No Problem is that it has to be done all at once. There is no gradual way to approach it. You have to decide that from this moment forward you will not allow yourself to relate to anything as a problem – at least during meditation. From that point on you simply adopt the position that nothing is a problem – no matter what. Simple.

What often happens in the name of having no problem is that we keep catching ourselves in the middle of believing that there is something wrong and then reminding ourselves that nothing is wrong. This isn't quite it because the only reason we would need to remind ourselves that nothing is wrong would be because we believed that there was something wrong with forgetting that.

It is easy for this meditation practice to become all about remembering that there is no problem. But this is not the practice of remembering that you don't have a problem. It is the practice of not having a problem no matter what you think. So, it needs to be OK with us if it feels like something is wrong.

So, what do you do in meditation when you realize that you have been lost in the belief that something is wrong? Nothing. Once you realize that you were lost in a problem, you aren't lost anymore and so there's nothing you have to do except have no problem with having been lost.

Every problem is just another voice in your head telling you that you have a problem. Those voices are often followed by other voices that tell you not to listen to the problem voice. And still other voices start having a problem with all the voices. "You shouldn't be thinking. You're not supposed to be thinking. You're not really doing it. I knew you couldn't do it. You'll never be able to do it." Sound familiar?

Eventually, you realize that every problem is just another voice in your head telling you that you have a problem. When you realize that those voices are not you, that you are the one who hears the voices not the one speaking, something completely different happens. At that point, you stop caring about what any of the voices are saying. The voices may fall away, or they may not. It doesn't matter to you because you are free either way.

I once had the opportunity to do a meditation retreat for two months. I was meditating from four in the morning until ten at night. I had always had difficulty with falling asleep in meditation and during this retreat I was determined not to fall asleep.

One day, at the beginning of the second month, I was meditating and I was very tired. It can be almost torturous to meditate when you're very tired. Your eyes burn, your head hurts, and you feel nervous tension running through your body.

As I was sitting in this very difficult situation, a thought went through my mind. It said, "you're not really tired." And for some reason, in that instant, something profound happened; I realized that I wasn't tired. I just happened to be looking through a tired body, but I was completely awake anyway. In fact, I had never been anything other than completely awake. It is not even possible to be less than completely awake.

Awareness is always on, and there is no dimmer switch. You can't turn it down. Sometimes what you are aware of is a very tired body, but you are still awake.

When I went to sleep that night, I felt my body fall asleep but I was still there. Everything went black and I couldn't feel my body. I was just floating in space. I thought, "This is cool. My body fell asleep and I'm still awake."

Then a dream happened. It was like someone turned the lights on and I was in the middle of a dream. I thought, "I'm dreaming and I'm still awake. This is so cool." Then the dream went away as if the light had been turned off, and I was floating in empty space again.

Then another dream appeared and disappeared. Then another. When my alarm went off in the morning, my body woke up and I thought, "I'm still here." I started to wonder, who was asleep? Who is awake now? And what is the difference between meditating and just walking around if I am here all the time anyway?

The next night, the same thing happened. My body fell asleep and I was still here. I thought, "Oh, this is cool." And I spent the whole next day marveling at the fact that I'm always here and always awake even in sleep. The next night my body fell asleep and I remained awake again. Then I started to worry that this might not be healthy and the night after that I fell asleep and lost consciousness. When I woke up in the morning, I was relieved at first and then disappointed.

What I realized from that experience will stay with me forever. We are always awake no matter how it seems. We were awake before we were born, and we will continue to be awake after we die. Whether we are aware of it or not doesn't really matter. It is still true even when we don't realize it.

The Practice of No Problem is about being with everything exactly the way it already is. Most of us live in a struggle with the way things are. As long as our energy is wrapped up in a struggle with the way things are, we are not available for anything more. If we keep ourselves relentlessly busy struggling nothing changes.

If you learn to accept the way things are, your energy is free, your attention is free, and you are available to experience things that you couldn't imagine before. That is when you become profoundly available to evolve. When we learn to stop struggling with the way things are, we are available to be lifted into higher possibilities.

That is what this book is all about.

CHAPTER SEVEN
THE PRACTICE OF NO PROBLEM IS
NOT SPIRITUAL BYPASSING

In the last chapter I explained how I teach meditation by asking people to sit still and not make a problem out of whatever experience they happen to be having. I always explain that what we experience during meditation doesn't really matter because the value of meditation is not measured in terms of the experience we happen to have during the practice.

When people have difficulty with this way of meditating, it's usually because they assume that, to have no problem, they have to feel like they have no problem. So, without realizing it, they try to manipulate their experience into one that they find pleasurable or at least acceptable.

This is when people might start to wonder if they are engaging in what is sometimes called spiritual bypassing, which means using our spiritual practice to avoid feeling bad. In fact, they are indeed practicing spiritual bypassing, but they are not doing The Practice of No Problem.

When we feel good it's easy to have no problem, but when we feel bad it's hard. In fact, most of us, most of the time, believe that in order to have no problem we have to feel good.

One of the most important things that any of us can learn is that feeling bad does not mean that something is wrong. If something is wrong, it means that things are not the way they should be. We've been raised in a culture that tells us that we should feel good. So, when we feel bad, we naturally assume that something is wrong.

But everyone feels bad sometimes. Yes, we all want to feel good, but that doesn't mean that we shouldn't feel bad. Feeling bad is a part of life. True spiritual practice is not about avoiding pain. It is about embracing all of life.

As I already mentioned, spiritual bypassing occurs when we use our spiritual work as a means of avoiding things that make us uncomfortable. The danger, of course, is that we avoid dealing with psychological issues or dysfunctional situations because they are uncomfortable for us to face.

I think you could really see spiritual bypassing as part of a larger phenomenon that we could call emotional bypassing in general. The root cause of emotional bypassing is our desire to feel good and not to feel bad.

Yes, you can use The Practice of No Problem to emotionally bypass, but you can also use drugs or alcohol, financial acquisition, sex, or almost anything else. I even have a psychologist friend who talks about how people will even use psychotherapy as a form of emotional bypassing.

Ultimately, almost anything can be used as an excuse not to face life's challenges. If our primary motive is feeling good, then we will inevitably find ways of avoiding feeling bad whenever we can.

True spiritual practices are not designed for the purpose of emotional bypassing. They are designed to liberate us – not from pain but from the need to feel good in order to be OK. Real spiritual practice should increase our capacity to face the challenging aspects of life not give us an excuse to escape them.

Don't get me wrong. We do discover a deep source of inner peace and contentment through spiritual practice, but the contentment that we find though The Practice of No Problem for instance points to an ease of being that is always present, even when we feel bad.

You can't measure the quality of your meditation based on how you feel during meditation. How you feel during meditation doesn't tell you much of anything. I'll be honest with you. I don't usually feel that great when I meditate.

Sure, sometimes in meditation I have expansive openings into abiding peace or blissful realizations of deeper truths, but a lot of the time I'm just sitting with a mind that tells me I should be doing something else. In meditation, I feel antsy and uncomfortable more often than I feel light, happy, and free.

In spite of this, I remain content because I know that how I feel during meditation doesn't tell me anything about the strength of my practice.

How I am able to show up in life is where I see the value of my practice. Let me use a dramatic example to make this point clear.

Six years ago, I got a call from the local hospital. My wife had been in a head-on collision with an 18-wheel tractor trailer and they told me I should come to the hospital immediately. They wouldn't give me any more information over the phone.

I was in no shape to drive so a friend took me to the hospital. As we drove, I could feel the panic rising up in my body. I couldn't control it. I was shaking all over. I was so scared. My mind kept telling me that my beautiful wife might already be dead, or in a coma, or horribly disfigured. In that moment I didn't practice having no problem. That would be ludicrous.

But I also wasn't entirely swallowed up by the panic. I remained present. I saw what was happening and I realized that I didn't know what I was going to find at the hospital, but whatever it was I knew I was going to deal with it.

As I sat in the car a question came to me. If my wife is dead or in a coma will that mean that life is bad? I considered it and realized that, no, life would still be good. My life might be terrible, but life itself would be good in spite of my horrifying misfortune.

At that point, I felt the panic subside. The universe was going to be OK no matter how difficult things got for me.

I wasn't challenged beyond that. I got to the hospital to find my wife alive. Her ankle was shattered and she had cuts and bruises all over, but she was going to live.

The strength of my practice can't be measured by how bored or uncomfortable I get when I meditate. It can be measured by the degree to which I don't lose myself under challenging circumstances.

My wife's story is much more remarkable than mine.

After the accident she found herself trapped inside a pile of twisted metal. She couldn't move a muscle. Can you imagine the temptation to panic?

She realized that this was likely to be the end of her life and she was determined to die with grace and dignity. She didn't kick and scream. She started breathing deeply, consciously willing herself to relax.

Soon a man stopped and reached in through the window of the car and held her head until the fire trucks arrived.

For 45 minutes she heard the sound of metal grinding as they cut the car away from her body and, the whole time, she maintained her breathing and her calm.

I wish I could say that I would be able to maintain composure like my wife under similar circumstances, but I won't know unless it happens.
The Practice of No Problem is not about emotional bypassing. It is not about pretending that having your wife injured, or your body trapped in wreckage, is OK.

It is about realizing the inherent goodness of life so deeply that you are ready to deal with anything that happens, no matter how difficult it is, with grace and dignity and presence of mind.

When we practice having no problem, we discover a depth of consciousness below all the problems. We realize that pain is not a problem, fear is not a problem, boredom is not a problem. These are all part of life and we can handle them if we have the wherewithal to stay connected to the reality of what is happening and not avoid it.

The Practice of No Problem is about gaining the strength of character and the presence of mind to be with life however it shows up.

I am not free of my tendencies for emotionally bypassing. I avoid pain and seek pleasure more often than I care to mention. And meditation alone does not ensure that I will be available to face all of the uncomfortable places inside myself. I get support for that when I need it. I regularly work with people who help me face things I might otherwise want to avoid and I recommend you do the same.

The trust in life that I've found in meditation provides the solid ground from which I can embrace all of life, and in one very challenging circumstance, I discovered that when push came to shove, I didn't shrink from the pain of existence. I was ready to deal with it whatever it was.

I am passionate about meditation because it supports us to live with dignity and grace even when challenged.

CHAPTER EIGHT
MEDITATION WITHOUT PRACTICE

Commonly we refer to meditation as a practice. I think this is a bad idea.

Practice is something you do now so that you will be able to perform better in the future when it really counts. You practice piano now so you will play well during your recital. You practice football now so you will play well in the game.

When we think of meditation as a practice we consciously or unconsciously start relating to it as something that is preparatory. Meditation – at least the way I see it – is not preparatory.

I define meditation as the immediate recognition of liberated awareness followed by a prolonged period of resting in that awareness.

First of all, meditation is the immediate recognition of liberated awareness.

Immediate means without mediation, without anything coming in between.

That means no following the breath, no repeating a mantra, no visualization of sacred symbols – nothing but the immediate recognition that your awareness is already free.

Of course, following the breath, repeating a mantra, or visualizing sacred symbols can lead us to a direct recognition of liberated awareness, but I would say that the real meditation doesn't start until then.

So how do we have an immediate recognition of liberated awareness? Well, if it is truly an immediate recognition then you must be having it already right now.

Yes, right now. The awareness that you have, the one that is reading these words is already free. That means that the person you are right now, as you read these words, is also already free.

There is already nothing wrong, nowhere to go, and nothing you need to do to make anything different than it is.

The trick is just leaving it at that. Don't think about, don't try to understand it. Just accept the truth of freedom and see what happens.

I'm on fire to share this mystery of awakening because it changes everything without changing anything.

Don't try to understand it. Just accept it. You are free. Free is what you are. There is no way that you could ever be limited, constrained, or stopped.

You expand infinitely in all directions. You exist at all times in all places – forever always everywhere.

Part of you will say, "but it doesn't feel that way." And that doesn't matter.

Being free doesn't depend on feeling free.

Free is what you are no matter how you feel. That is what makes it so unimaginably immediate!

Don't try to understand it. Just accept it and see what happens.

Over time, the way that I teach meditation has changed dramatically because I realize that, if I give too much instruction, people assume that there is something they need to understand.

If we want to be free, there is nothing we need to understand because free is what we already are.

I get so excited about the miracle of freedom that I could write about it forever – but it will be better for you if I don't.

CHAPTER NINE
THE IMMEDIACY OF MEDITATION

There is a magic to the practice of meditation that many practitioners never discover because we only find it when we eliminate time from the equation. You can call this the discovery of radical immediacy and it is the central insight of the Hindu tradition of Advaita Vedanta that I was initiated into, and the Dzogchen teachings of Tibetan Buddhism.

The secret to this profound approach to practice is the realization that true meditation is not something that happens in time. It happens instantaneously, the moment you decide to let go. It doesn't matter if you sit for twenty minutes or two hours, the meditation always occurs in the very first instant. Everything after that is *just sitting* as any Zen master will tell you.

When you sit in meditation you simply let go. You just drop all attempts to control, alter or manipulate your experience and let everything be exactly as it is. As the Sufi mystic Rumi put it, "close your eyes and surrender."

If in meditation you find yourself engaged in the activity of trying to let go, you are, in actuality, still holding on. Pick up a pen in your hand and then let it go. How long does it take? If you open your hand slowly, it could take an hour before the pen drops. That doesn't mean that you were letting go for an hour. It means you were holding on, albeit less and less, for an hour before letting go.

We often, without realizing it, approach meditation the same way we approach everything else in life — as an accomplishment to be achieved.

At the start of meditation, we see ourselves as separate from some higher state of consciousness that we must work toward through the practice.

By imagining ourselves as somehow *not there,* we are inadvertently causing our own bondage. Spiritual freedom is not a goal that we attain in the future. It is the truth of our true nature now. Free is what we are.

The only thing that keeps us from realizing it is our own insistence that we are not.

True meditation is not an activity designed to liberate you. It is the practice of freedom itself. The goal is freedom and the practice is to be free. No distance needs to be traveled and no time passes in this journey to where you already are.

This is the realization of radical immediacy. The magic begins as soon as we choose to be free by simply allowing everything to be exactly the way it already is.

Suddenly, we realize that we have slipped out of time. We have become liberated from the relentless march of passing moments.

It is impossible to describe in words, but it is as if you are nowhere and everywhere simultaneously. You still see every thought, every feeling, every sensation, but you are not inside them any longer.

As you continue to rest in this magical space beyond time, the passing show of arising experience becomes less and less captivating of your attention. Gradually, you become aware of the utterly invisible infinite space that all experience arises in.

I believe that this experience of trans-sensual perception is what inspires spiritual passages that speak to being blind but seeing everywhere.

Practicing meditation in this way initiates us into the mystery of being.

Once we taste the invisible infinitude that engulfs us, we realize that it is not just empty space. It is a living being – the ultimate source of wisdom and love in the universe. It is not dead. It is alive and it lives through us.

From this moment on, we feel compelled to become an ever more perfect channel for the manifestation of this universal heart and mind. We recognize in a way that can perhaps best be described in the words made famous in the West by the Indian sage Nisargadatta when he proclaimed, "I am that."

If we are so lucky that our identification with the small self yields to the recognition of who we really are, our spiritual orientation will flip on its head. We are no longer interested in trying to get anywhere, we only want to be more and more of who and what we already are.

CHAPTER TEN
THE DELICATE ART OF DOING
ABSOLUTELY NOTHING

The first time I was engulfed by the realization of the inherent perfection of being was during a sixty-day meditation retreat under the guidance of my spiritual teacher at the time. As I sat from morning until evening following the simple instruction "let everything be as it is," I found myself transported to an experience of consciousness that I had no way to anticipate.

Sitting hour after hour with my legs crossed, I made supreme effort to follow those simple instructions. I simply allowed whatever I was experiencing to be exactly as it was without making any effort at all to do anything. The goal was to truly do nothing and resist the temptation to engage in any way with any part of my experience.

It was a practice of perfect passivity that literally asked me to not do anything at all.

As the hours of meditation became days of meditation, I saw over and over again how I would catch myself in the earnest effort of trying to do nothing. Every time I would catch myself, I would realize that *trying to do nothing* is still doing something – and doing something is not doing nothing. So, with each realization I would stop doing something and start doing nothing.

After relentless hours spent revolving through this cycle of entrapment and escape, I began to realize that every time I *stopped doing something*, I was doing something. Stopping doing something was still doing something, and the goal was to do nothing. If stopping doing something was still doing something, then how could I do nothing? I spent prolonged periods locked in the mental gymnastics of trying to do nothing, while realizing over and over again that trying to do nothing was still doing something. It was supremely frustrating, like trying to look at the back of your eyeballs. It seemed that the spiritual physics would not allow me to do nothing.

Eventually, I realized something that was so obvious that I couldn't see it before. If the instruction is to let everything be as it is, I literally couldn't fail. Absolutely everything that happens is already the way it is, and there is no reason to do anything about it.

Whenever I realized that I had spent the last twenty minutes locked in an imaginary struggle to let everything be as it is – well, that was simply the way it was. In the moment of realizing it, there was nothing more to do except see what happened next. Anything that you experience and anything that you do will always be the way it is. Meditation is not different from just being – it is a practice of perfect acceptance of everything.

Once I realized this, my experience of meditation changed completely even though nothing was different. I was still struggling in all the same ways. I was still having breakthrough experiences of bliss and illumination, still living through prolonged, tormenting bouts of doubt and frustration. Nothing was different except it all stopped bothering me.

It was so obvious. The instruction is to allow everything to be the way it is, and the way it is is already the way it is. Sometimes we're sitting quietly aware; other times we get lost in thought and struggle; and then sometimes we wake up from being lost in thought. That is the cycle of consciousness that we experience all the time. That is the way it is.

The awakening of this meditation practice comes with the realization that no matter what I experience, it is the way it is already, and there is nothing I could do to make it otherwise. No matter what appears to be happening, everything will always already be the way it is, including thinking that it is not. At this point in my meditation, my effort to practice came to an end. I stopped feeling like there was anything I could do. I stopped wanting anything to be different from the way that it already was.

Everything was different, and nothing had changed.

In the way I teach meditation, you come to a place where you stop needing to do anything because you accept that everything is already the way it is and there is nothing you need to do, or even could do, to change that. Life is already whole, complete and full just the way it is, no matter how it is. This realization is the essence of spiritual freedom.

CHAPTER ELEVEN
RESTING IN THE SPACE IN-BETWEEN

The spiritual path, in a sense, is a process of forgetting yourself to remember yourself - or better said, forgetting your false self to remember your True Self. In this chapter, we will explore a miraculous state of consciousness that we can either fall into accidentally or learn to rest in consciously. It is in this magical awareness that the self-forgetting and the self-remembering often occur. This transformational space in consciousness is somewhere between our normal wakeful state and our sleep state. It is a middle place and, when we fall into it accidentally, we sometimes wonder if we're falling asleep.

Any of us who meditate have almost certainly experienced meditation sessions where we've gotten sleepy and nodded off. As a meditation teacher, I've always hedged a bit with my answers to the inevitable question that arises around this perplexing issue - should I make an effort to stay awake? On the one hand, I recognize the importance of staying alert and awake. On the other hand, some of my most powerful spiritual experiences occurred in moments when I thought I was falling asleep.

For instance, once on retreat, I kept feeling my head starting to nod backward. Each time, I would dutifully jerk it forward again and stiffen up. Eventually, I decided that I would let myself fall asleep and see what happened. So, the next time I started to fall backward, I didn't stop myself and guess what? I didn't fall off the chair! Instead, my consciousness fell right out of the back of my head. I was literally aware from behind my own head and my awareness stayed that way for three days. I had mind-shattering insights during those days that propelled me forward on the path, and none of it would have happened if I hadn't taken the risk of falling asleep.

A second example occurred on a different retreat when I was very tired and meditating late at night. Actually, I was struggling to stay alert as opposed to actually meditating. I kept tensing up to stay awake until, at one point, it suddenly occurred to me that I wasn't really tired. At that moment, I fell into a place in consciousness that was perfectly awake and aware even though it was aware through a very tired body.

For three days and three nights, I couldn't lose consciousness. I was aware all day; I was aware as my body fell asleep at night; and I was aware as my mind drifted in and out between dream states and deep empty sleep. In the morning, my alarm would go off and I would watch my body wake up. I was experiencing a place in consciousness that was always constantly aware throughout all the changes that my mind and body were going through. I knew that this consciousness was who I really was; that I had been that before I was born and would be that again once this body was gone. My existential fear of death was gone and it hasn't ever returned.

Experiences like these are why I'm careful about how I instruct people around sleep in meditation. On the one hand, we need to develop concentration by making the effort to stay awake. At the same time, there might be times when what feels like sleep is actually the dawning of a deeper awakening.

In the book, *The Spiritual Teachings of Ramana Maharshi*, I discovered that my experiences were congruent with what the great sage Ramana taught. There are several passages in the book that speak to exactly this issue in ways that confirmed my hesitations about condemning sleep in practice.

In one of these passages, someone explains that, in doing their practice for long periods of time, they fall into a state like sleep and wonder if they should wake themselves up and start again?

Ramana says, "Like sleep, that is right. It is the natural state. Because you are now associated with the ego, you consider that the natural state is something which interrupts your work. So, you must have the experience repeatedly until you realize that it is your natural state. You will then find that practice is extraneous, but still it will go on automatically. Your present doubt is due to that false identity, namely, of identifying yourself with the mind that does practice."

What Ramana is explaining is, because we're identified with the mind in its normal wakeful state as who we are, we don't realize that this more dreamy state is actually our natural state of being. To Ramana, this is the state of true meditation and it is a return to our True Self.

66

The way I understand it, this sleep-like state is what we experience as we begin to forget our separate sense of self or ego in meditation. This self-forgetting places us in a state of pure consciousness, which is meditation. If we don't recognize this, we will keep bringing ourselves back into the more familiar wakeful conscious state and we will continually return to experiencing ourselves as an ego meditating. If, instead, we can allow ourselves to drift off and come to rest in the space of self-forgetfulness, our practice will continue but we won't be aware of doing it anymore. This is the doorway to the revelation of our true self.

At the beginning of this chapter I said that this in-between consciousness could be entered into and sustained accidentally or deliberately. Now, I want to explore what can happen when you learn to consciously hold yourself in that delicate space of awareness by sharing a particularly dramatic instance of self-remembering that occurred during a two-month-long meditation retreat I did.

On that retreat, I was exploring how to embrace an impossible combination of opposites, where I was focused, concentrated and alert on one hand, and relaxed, at ease, and restful on the other. That is the magic combination of opposites that constitutes true meditation. It is the space where the opposing poles of concentration and relaxation combine to make miracles happen.

During this retreat, I spent many hours of meditation learning to sit restfully in this in-between place for longer and longer periods of time and, as a result, I was experiencing a tremendous deepening of my practice. The deepening would start as a sinking feeling, as if I was floating downward through murky depths toward the ocean floor. As the deepening continued, I became more and more relaxed, at peace, and largely withdrawn from external sensations, and yet, at the same time, the experience of awareness became tremendously vivid, vibrant and alive.

In some traditions, this unique combination of qualities is referred to as the perfect middle place between all pairs of opposites. I've also heard it simply called betweenness. By cultivating this profound inner space, you are perfectly attentive without focusing on anything. What makes this posture so magical is the unique combination of being completely energized and totally disengaged at the same time. It is a state of pure potentiality and, if you sit there long enough, something extraordinary will inevitably happen.

During one particular meditation session, as I was resting in that beautiful space, something amazing did happen. At some point, the deepening slowed down and then stopped as if I had gently settled onto the ocean floor. I was simply resting in pure potential with nowhere to go, nothing to do, and nothing missing. It's impossible to tell how long I was resting there, because there was no sense of time at all.

At some point, I began to feel an outward flowing energy. It was a delightful sensation of energy from the center of my being rolling outwards toward and beyond my edges. I was meditating with my eyes gently open gazing downward toward the floor. I wasn't paying attention to what I was looking at, but I couldn't help noticing when the floor started moving away from me.

At first, I thought that I was floating toward the ceiling, but then I realized I was still sitting on the floor. I was just getting bigger. Eventually, I was so big that my head was at the height of the ceiling and I was looking straight-out at the rafters. Then, my head passed through the ceiling and I was outside above the building.

I kept growing and growing. I could see the town far below me, and then the hills and valleys for miles around. Eventually, I could see the globe of the Earth until it shrunk down to become just a tiny dot. Finally, I saw all the stars of the universe inside myself. The expansion stopped and I experienced the cosmic delight of the universe. It was the most perfect state of wholeness and completeness that I had ever experienced. I cannot truly describe what it felt like, because no words can contain it.

In the midst of that bliss, I realized that this was a place I had known intimately when I was just a little boy. I finally remembered something that I had forgotten for nearly forty years. What I remembered was that, at the age of three or four, I would lock myself in my parents' bathroom and look into the full-length mirror that hung on the door. As I stood perfectly still, staring into my own eyes, I would grow until I was the size of the universe and I would rest there for a while in a fully exalted state of being. When I would eventually return to the bathroom, I would simply unlock the door and go my way.

I have no idea how many times I did this as a child but now, on retreat as an adult, I clearly remembered the last time I had gone to the mirror only to discover that I couldn't do it anymore. No matter how hard I stared into my own eyes nothing happened. I was stuck. I couldn't expand anymore and, evidently, I soon forgot that I ever could.

The expansion I experienced years later on retreat was identical to my childhood experiences and, just like when I was a boy, at some point I began to shrink again and the globe of the Earth slowly became visible against the background of stars. As I slowly settled all the way back down to my position sitting cross-legged on the floor, I felt perfectly content and utterly amazed at what I had remembered.

Suddenly, my lifelong obsession with spiritual pursuit made perfect sense. Of course, I never felt content with my conventional life. Of course, I went to see teachers, learned techniques, did countless hours of practice, and lived in a spiritual community for twenty years. What else could I do? I needed to find my way home.

One of the false assumptions about ourselves that many of us may be holding onto is the belief that we haven't experienced the truth of who we are. Maybe that isn't true. I wonder, how many times have you already experienced the miraculous truth of who you are and forgotten about it like I did?

I believe that those of us following the spiritual path are not being driven by what we haven't experienced but, rather, by what we have experienced and forgotten about. It makes sense if you think about it. Where would you get all the energy to follow a spiritual path if you didn't already know what was there to find?

I ask again, how many times do you think you might have already experienced the ultimate glory of who you are and forgotten about it?

The next time you meditate, see what happens if you sit in that perfect middle place between all pairs of opposites and rest in the pure possibility you find there.

CHAPTER TWELVE
YOU DON'T NEED A SPIRITUAL EXPERIENCE TO WAKE UP

How many people are chasing after spiritual experiences? How many meditators are sitting hour after hour hoping to have their minds blown? How many people go to see gurus and teachers in the hopes of getting struck by a bolt of illumination that will knock them into a permanently awakened state?

I bet there are lots of them. I was definitely one for many years. I was a very hard-working seeker. I spent tens of thousands of hours on my meditation cushion. I sat so still through extremes of pain that tears ran down my cheeks. I stayed up all night doing physical spiritual practices that damaged my knees and shoulders. I repeated mantras in my head over and over until I couldn't think of anything else.

And yes, I had spiritual experiences – lots of them. I've experienced white hot light rushing up from the base of my spine straight through the top of my head. I've been knocked into an awareness that was so wide open that I forgot how to lose consciousness even while my body slept through the night. And I've experienced myself so expanded that I could see the stars and galaxies of the universe running through my body.

I've had countless experiences and each one eventually faded until all that remained was a memory of a past event. It didn't stick like I hoped it would. And each time, I got over my disappointment, shook off the loss, and got right back at it. Flying off to the next retreat ready to give even more of my energy to the quest.

In the end, after decades of seeking, I realized that I was putting too much emphasis on these experiences when the real prize had already been won. Sure, experiences help by expanding our awareness and transporting us to miraculous places. They give us experiential proof that something more exists beyond our ordinary day to day life. They inspire us and fuel our spiritual passion. Each experience we have leaves us more convinced and committed to awakening.

But these miraculous moments mislead us if we become convinced that we need them to be awake. Spiritual awakening is not an experience. It is not an energetic blast, or an expansion of consciousness. It is not anything that is not ours already. Spiritual awakening is a simple, often quiet, recognition of our own inherent freedom and expansive nature.

What we recognize in moments of true spiritual awakening is that we are already free. That means we are OK no matter what experience we happen to be having.

The reason spiritual experiences can mislead us is because they often leave us convinced that we need to be having that kind of experience in order to be free.

When I teach meditation, I'm really teaching spiritual freedom. I am not teaching a technique. There is no visualization to focus on, no mantra to recite, no breath to follow, nothing. All I ask is that you sit and be OK with whatever experience you happen to have no matter what it is.

We've been trained to assume that our state of being is determined by the quality of our mind. If we are having an experience of happiness, then we are happy. If we are having an experience of frustration, then we are frustrated. And when we are having an experience of anxiety, then we are anxious. We assume that the quality of our experience tells us who we are.

So, our state of being is all over the map, happy this moment, sad the next, on top of the world today, down in the dumps tomorrow. Naturally, when we start our spiritual search, part of what we are seeking for is some relief from all this inner bouncing around.

What we are searching for is inner peace and tranquility – and dramatic spiritual experiences can totally stop our mind and leave us feeling amazing for a few minutes, hours, days or weeks. The downside is that too often we conclude that we need an experience like that in order to be free and we develop a spiritual addiction to them.

Many of us, myself included, spent years doing ever more extreme forms of spiritual practice in order to trigger more and more experiences, without realizing that we didn't need them. Sure, they propelled us into a vast expanse of inner space, but it's the fact that the expanse exists that really matters not the experience that happened to get us there.

The inner peace that we find in the wake of dramatic spiritual openings was already there. That deep and abiding space of clarity and wonder is what it feels like to be alive before we become convinced that life is defined by the transitory experiences of our mind.

Dramatic spiritual experiences can dislodge our attention from the compulsive fixation on the content of thought and feeling. This feels so liberating because we've been trained to have our awareness constantly glued to our habitual experience of mind. A never-ending parade of thoughts, feelings, sensations, emotions, images, fantasies, fears, worries and concerns consume almost all of our attention each and every day.

Dramatic spiritual experiences allow our attention to drift beyond the limits of mind into the ocean of consciousness that was always surrounding us. Once we become aware of that ocean, some contraction deep inside our being releases and we begin to expand outward in every direction.

But, and here is the whole point, you don't need a dramatic experience to become aware of the ocean of consciousness that is all around you. All you need to do is release your attention from the confines of mind. Expanding into the great mystery beyond the known happens naturally. It doesn't take any effort.

What takes effort is holding your attention on something as small and limited as a human mind when your awareness naturally wants to spread out infinitely. We don't have any idea how much effort we're making to limit ourselves until we release. Suddenly we see how hard we've been working to keep our attention focused in such a narrow way.

So, when I teach meditation, I don't teach any particular technique – no visualization to pay attention to, no mantra to repeat, no breath to follow. Instead, I encourage people to just let go. Stop trying to do anything, including trying to meditate. If awakening is truly our natural state, then it's already here, and there couldn't be anything we need to do to get there – even have a dramatic spiritual experience.

If you're someone who's done a lot of practice and had lots of experiences already, that's wonderful. If you're just getting started or haven't had any big experiences yet, it really doesn't matter. What's yours is yours already anyway. That deep and abiding space of clarity and wonder does not belong to anyone, it is the ocean we are all floating in. Don't worry it's waiting for you already.

CHAPTER THIRTEEN
THE SUN IS ALWAYS SHINING

As we discussed in the last chapter, those of us who sincerely seek for spiritual liberation and awakening are most likely hoping to have a spiritual experience or opening that is powerful enough, deep enough, or long-lasting enough that it becomes our permanent state of consciousness.

Unfortunately, this hope might just be the only obstacle standing in the way of our true awakening.

You see, we've been taught to think about spiritual awakening the wrong way. We've been given a model that is faulty and that all but guarantees we won't find the fulfillment we're looking for.

We've been taught that the holy grail of the spiritual path is having an awakening experience that becomes permanent. We've been taught to seek for an experience that sticks.

We've had spiritual experiences, maybe even powerful and profound ones that have lasted for a few moments, a few hours or longer, but they always seem to disappear in the end leaving us busy searching for more.

So, at some point along the way, we decide that we need to spend time on retreat to be able to practice long enough and intensely enough to have an experience so explosive that it shifts our consciousness into a permanently awakened state.

We go on retreat. Maybe for a weekend, or a week, or a month or longer. We have spiritual experiences, maybe many of them, perhaps very powerful ones, and yet they all eventually recede from awareness.

So, we go back on retreat, each time resolved to give it everything we have – determined to open so wide that we will never close down again.

How do I know? Because I did exactly this, time and time again for over twenty years.

Then one day something did happen – but it wasn't anything like what I was hoping for.

I sat down to the first practice of the very first day of yet another twenty-day retreat. As I walked up to my cushion, I thought about how I was going to be more still, more focused, more intent, and more receptive than ever before. I was ready for this to be the big one.

I sat down and the bell rang to start the first meditation, and something happened that I absolutely didn't expect.

As soon as I heard the bell sound to start off the meditation, I realized that I just didn't have it in me. I couldn't do this retreat harder than ever before because I just didn't have the energy for another round.

Initially, I thought something was terribly wrong. I started to imagine that I may have lost my passion for spiritual freedom and enlightenment.

But as I sat there for a minute, I realized that wasn't it at all.

The reason I didn't have the energy to pursue any more awakening experiences was because I didn't need any more.

Why? Because I was already convinced. I knew that the glory that I had experienced so many times before had always been, and would always be, the deepest part of me – even when I was not experiencing it directly.

Suddenly, I realized that I didn't need any more spiritual experiences because I already knew the truth of who I was and I didn't need any more experiences to remind me.

I can't tell you how free that felt. Imagine a moment of recognizing that everything is already perfect, always has been and always will be – because at the deepest level of our being we are always whole, complete, and profoundly fulfilled.

I stayed on retreat and it was the best meditation retreat of my life, because I didn't want or need to get anything from it. I was absolutely free to just sit hour after hour and be perfectly content with everything exactly as it was.

I spent hours simply absorbed in the experience of sitting still and watching the parade of thoughts and feelings pass by the mind's eye. Occasionally, my spirit would mysteriously lift into an unprompted experience of elation and revelation. Then it would gently return to just sitting.

It was all perfect. I was sitting in a continuous state of unbroken trust and contentment.

As a teacher of awakening and meditation, all I want is to make this magnificent possibility available to others.

I suppose you might get there by chasing more spiritual experiences, but that could take another ten or twenty years.

Instead, I teach that the secret to awakening is realizing that what we discover in our spiritually heightened moments is simply the truth of how things already are.

The goal of awakening is not to have an experience that sticks. It is to recognize the true freedom that is the natural state of our own consciousness before it gets distorted by fear, desire, or the inevitable wounds of life.

Our spiritual experiences do not reveal a future possibility. They show us the way things already are.

The goal is not an experience that sticks. It is learning to trust that the miracle you discover in your most profound revelations of truth is always already here. It is like realizing that the Sun is always shining even when it's cloudy. The Sun is only visible to us on a clear day, but that doesn't make us doubt whether the Sun is still there on a cloudy day. We know the Sun is there even when it is cloudy.

In the same way, it is possible to come to a place where we know that the spaciousness of an open heart and mind is always there even when our attention is distracted by fear, doubt or self-concern.

If you find the courage to give up any investment in having an experience that sticks, you will find yourself living in an ongoing recognition of the miraculous truth of who you already are.

CHAPTER FOURTEEN
TANTRA, NON-DUALITY AND THE PRACTICE OF NO PROBLEM

In the traditions of the East, a spiritual path is considered Tantric when its goal is to bring about the direct recognition of the immediate availability of our boundless nature. Tantra and Tantric paths do not see the world, the mind, or anything else as an obstacle to this awakening because every aspect of reality is seen as inherently sacred. The divine can be found everywhere at anytime. In a Tantric path we do not leave the world to find heaven. We find Heaven in our experience of the world as it already is.

In his magnificent book *An Introduction to Tantra*, the great Lama Yeshe points out that in Buddhism all approaches to spiritual fulfillment fall into two categories, Sutra or Sutrayana, and Tantra or Tantrayana. Sutrayana refers to paths that offer a gradual process aimed at eliminating the obstacles that keep us from realizing fulfillment. Tantric paths, on the other hand, assume that fulfillment is already ours from the start so there is no need to go through any process to find it.

In this sense, I see the attitude of Tantra in the good news of Christianity. In the story of Jesus's ministry, his twelve disciples are sent out after his death to spread the good news. The good news simply stated is: "The Kingdom of Heaven is here." This news meant that there was no longer any need to wait for fulfillment until after we left this world. Heaven could be found here on Earth. This is also the core message of the Eastern Tantric traditions.

Tantric paths are supremely direct and immediate. My own spiritual path was Tantric in this broad sense, although it was not Buddhist, and was not labeled as such by my teacher. I was initiated in a Hindu tradition called Advaita Vedanta and, at least the way it was introduced to me, it is a deeply Tantric path in exactly the sense that I've been describing.

The foundational premise of Advaita Vedanta is that we are already whole and complete, because the essence of reality is already whole and complete. Our nature is boundless and free because that is the nature of reality itself and we are not separate from it. The Advaita tradition aims at liberating us from any and all assumptions of separation or deficiency, because these assumptions are the only thing that keeps us from realiz-

85

ing the boundless freedom that is always already the nature of who we are.

Advaita Vedanta, as I learned it, is a path that has no path. In fact, it rests on a strong assertion that there is no path and could never be a path, because the destination is always already here. This insistence on no separation between you and ultimate fulfillment is the essence of any Tantric path.

In many schools of Advaita Vedanta, meditation or any other form of spiritual practice is discouraged. Since we are already free, there is no need to do anything to get free. In fact, anything that you do in order to liberate yourself must be motivated by a delusional belief that you are not free already. Any belief we have in our own limitation is the only thing that keeps us from realizing our true boundless and unlimited nature.

The Practice of No Problem that I teach is a variation of the meditation practice I was initiated in. It is a supremely direct approach to awakening that can perhaps best be understood as a Tantric practice of Non-Duality.

Non-Duality means Oneness, or more literally "not-two." If the essence of reality is non-dual Oneness, then there could not possibly be a path to get there. Any path to Oneness would have to be separate from Oneness and that would mean two. That is why it is said that the path and the goal are one.

As we have already stated, when teaching The Practice of No Problem, I simply ask people to sit still and not make a problem out of anything. No matter what happens in the privacy of your own inner experience, you don't make a problem out of it. Even if you see your mind making a problem out of something, you don't make a problem out of that. It really is as simple as sitting down at the start of the meditation, remaining still during the meditation, and then getting up when the meditation period is over.

Literally nothing could be simpler, yet when we try, we often find that it is supremely difficult. The reason it is so challenging to have no problem is because it ultimately requires that we give up control and let go of any preferences we might have.

In this meditation, your experience is always assumed to be exactly what it should be. Ultimately, in order to truly have no problem, you must learn how to be perfectly content with exactly the way things are, no matter how they are, without exception.

This demand to be happy with things as they are is another reason why I see this meditation as Tantric in nature. Another core element of any Tantric practice is the belief that the energy of pleasure is not a hindrance to spiritual fulfillment that should be avoided. Pleasure, and our desire for it, is seen as a powerful energy that, when skillfully worked with, actually generates awakening.

The Practice of No Problem is the conscious practice of perfect contentment and unconditional happiness. When you decide to have no problem, you are consciously choosing to be content right now even when you feel uncomfortable.

This practice is challenging because it takes away any possibility of feeling justified in being dissatisfied with our experience. We all feel that we have the right to be dissatisfied and this practice only allows for perfect contentment. Of course, feelings of discontent do arise in meditation, but if they do the simple instructions would ask you to be perfectly content with being discontent. To me, learning to be content with being discontent is the secret to lasting happiness.

One of the miracles of meditation is the recognition that contentment is not just a feeling. We can be content even when we feel discontent. We can be happy even when we feel unhappy. I realize that this may sound nonsensical, but it is the key to spiritual freedom. As long as you believe that your contentment is dependent on having a particular feeling, you will always be chasing after that feeling.

When you realize what true contentment is, you can choose to be content anytime under any circumstances. In fact, the energetic shock of this recognition can be so powerful that it shifts your nervous system into a state of ongoing contentment. Not an ongoing feeling of contentment, but an ongoing sense of being at home and at peace no matter what you are experiencing.

In order to be perfectly content with everything as it is, even with feeling discontent, we have to give up all preference whatsoever. When we have no preference, we stop doing anything at all. To have no problem means to have no preference, and to have no preference means to do nothing because doing anything at all is always an expression of preference.

If we persist with the practice meticulously, we will eventually start to lose track of ourselves because we normally experience ourselves through our preferences - I like this, but not that, I want this, but not that, this makes me happy, this makes me unhappy, this is good, this is bad, my goal is over here, not over there -and on and on and on.

As all preferences fall away, we don't know who we are anymore. We are free from identity and self-concern. We have disappeared. This is the dissolution into emptiness that is the source of freedom that many spiritual paths describe. It takes tremendous courage to keep letting go once we start to feel our identity falling away. Only those who truly and deeply want to be free will be willing to keep going and let it all go.

What we discover when we let it all go is that we don't disappear in the way we feared we would. All of our ideas about who we are fall away, but even when we don't know anything about ourselves, we're still here. What we give up is any sense of separation from ourselves. We lose the external vantage point from which we have always known ourselves. We simply are who we are without knowing who we are. We are home.

We enter into a place where there is just experience and no one experiencing it. The sense of 'me' being someone who is separate from the experience I am having vanishes. There is a sense of total connection and boundless freedom. We extend in all directions simultaneously. We are nowhere and everywhere always at once. There is nothing we need to do because we are already home and always have been.

CHAPTER FIFTEEN
MEDITATION IS LIKE FALLING IN LOVE

We understand through metaphors. Falling in love is a great metaphor to help us understand the practice of meditation.

Language is a system that uses metaphors to clarify and reveal different aspects of reality. Words point to things or experiences. Generally, we assume that the language we use to describe things doesn't affect what they are.

But when we use words to describe something, especially something as subtle as meditation, the metaphors actually shape our experience of it. The metaphors we use to help us understand meditation orient us in particular ways. They open us to certain possibilities and close us to others.

The most common metaphor used to understand meditation is the metaphor of practice. The metaphor of practice can be very valuable in certain ways, while being problematic in others. The problem is that when we relate to meditation as a practice, it becomes something we use to improve our performance in the same way that we practice the piano in order to play better.

This is not the best way to think about meditation because meditation is not about performing better later. The metaphor of practice engages goal-oriented sensibilities and triggers our willfulness in ways that will not support the surrender that meditation is. Meditation is not something you get better at. It is not a skill to be developed. It is an act of surrender that demands the complete relinquishment of all willful effort to control or manipulate our experience.

A practice is something we do in order to improve. It is, as I already explained, an effort we make now in the hope of performing better later. I practice football so that I will perform better in the game. Practicing football or the piano is a means to an end. It is done for a purpose. Meditation is an end in itself. You don't meditate so that something will happen later. Meditation is its own goal.

If we think of meditation as a practice, we can easily start relating to it as a means to an end. It becomes something we do for a purpose. Often, we approach meditation in the hopes of having an experience of awakening, or attaining higher levels of peace, joy, and relaxation. If this is the case, our attention is focused on the future and our meditation practice pulls us away from the present moment.

When you are performing on stage, you are fully present because you know that this is the moment you have been preparing for. This level of presence is exactly what we want to bring to our meditation practice.

Holding our meditation as a practice can dull the vibrancy and immediacy of the present moment by holding us in spellbound anticipation of an event that we imagine will happen in the future.

This is diametrically opposed to what meditation is all about. Meditation asks us to let go of any habits that keep us fixated on the future. It is supposed to relieve us of any sense that we are living in the meantime prior to the main event. To the extent that we believe that what really matters will happen later, we will abide in a perpetually dissatisfied relationship to the present. This moment will always appear as deficient in comparison to some imagined more perfect future.

The purpose of meditation is to let go of the future and fall into a deep appreciation of the present. This instant, the one we are sharing right now, is the one that matters. This present moment is the only place where life actually happens. This moment is the one we want to pour all of your energy into, because it is the only moment there is.

Meditation is a total embrace of this very moment. In true meditation there is no holding back, no postponing, no conserving energy for the future. It is a total release into this very moment of being.

The metaphor of falling in love is exquisitely attuned to what meditation really is. By adopting the same inner sensitivity and receptivity that we experience when we fall in love, we discover the exact inner postures that allow us to give ourselves completely to the experience of the present moment. Meditation becomes the practice of falling in love with what is.

We have all had the experience of falling in love. When you fall in love, you enter into a particular state of consciousness. You become deeply attentive and aware of the beloved. You notice everything about them. In a very natural way, you are deeply open to them.

The whole event of falling in love feels like a celebration of life, a celebration of the other, and a celebration of yourself. There is no sense of waiting for something better to happen later. When we are falling in love, we know that this is what matters. This moment with the beloved is the moment that matters because it is the one we are actually sharing.

The quality of absorbed immediacy that we experience when falling in love is exactly the quality we want to cultivate in our meditation practice. It is the quality of being deeply in love with consciousness, infatuated with the miracle of being aware. As we sit in meditation, we allow ourselves to be deeply moved by the richness, the beauty, the tragedy, and the challenge of the human experience. By sitting and loving exactly what is, 'what is' continually opens, expands, awakens and transforms. We are overwhelmed with gratitude to be able to connect with this celebration of awakening.

Notice the difference in your experience of meditation when it is described in terms of falling in love rather than as a practice. When we emphasize practice, our orientation becomes more technical. We assume there is a right way to meditate that will allow us to achieve something. It creates a sense of separation from the goal. It encourages striving, which is exactly the habit of mind that meditation is an opportunity to let go of.

Meditation brings us into the direct recognition that this is it. This is the moment where life is actually happening. This is always that moment. Life always happens now, never in the future. The future only exists in our imagination. The past only exists in memory. Everything that is, is now. Even our memories of the past and our ideas about the future exist now, in the only moment that is. Life occurs in the present. Life is now. Meditation is the activity of being present to the reality of now. Meditation is falling in love with what is.

Meditation is like falling in love, and like falling in love, it is not something you *do*. It's something that *happens*. You can't make yourself fall in love; you find yourself falling in love. But, once you find yourself there, you have the choice to allow yourself to be taken by it or not. You can lean in the direction of love or you can choose to resist it.

In the same way, meditation is not something you do; it is something that happens. It is something you find yourself in and then you either choose to lean into it or resist it.

As you sit in meditation, see if you can find the meditation that is already happening - the meditation that was there before you sat down.
Can you find the meditation that has already begun? Can you find the place where you are always falling in love with this moment?

No matter what arises in your experience as you meditate, hold it with the arms of a lover; with joy, care, and deep tenderness. Meditate with a loving heart as well as a discerning mind. Care for the experience of this moment as if it were your dearest love.

Embrace this moment with everything you have. Accept it exactly the way it is. Be intimate with it. Experience it completely. Open into ever-greater receptivity and deeper presence. Be devoted in your love. Know that this is the only moment to give yourself to. It is the only moment you can fall in love with.

Allow yourself to be swept up in a divine communion with this moment exactly as it is. Whatever it is — joyful, painful, illuminating, confusing — know that this is it. Allow yourself to find the love of life that brought you into this world in the first place. Embrace that love as the only true meditation there is and allow it to take you into the unimaginable.

CHAPTER SIXTEEN
REMAINING STEADY THROUGH ANY STORM

One of the things we all yearn for is equanimity - the ability to remain steady through the inevitable ups and downs of life. Equanimity is the ability to not move and remain still and present at all times and under all circumstances.

Our physical stillness in meditation is a metaphor for inner stillness and equanimity. When we meditate, we find a deep inner stillness that initially feels like discovering something new. Eventually, however, we realize that we are discovering a part of ourselves that is always already perfectly still and always has been.

In deep meditation, we find that place that never moves. Ordinarily, we are so identified with the relentless movement of thought and feeling in consciousness that we make the mistake of thinking we're moving. Those thoughts and feelings are not us. By remaining very still in practice, we find a place where we are still and always have been still.

If in meditation we find ourselves getting blown around by our experience - reacting to thoughts and feelings that pass by - we too often assume that it is because we're not strong enough to be still. We start to believe that we haven't built up the right kinds of mental muscles to hold ourselves steady through the inevitable storms of experience that arise.

We don't gain equanimity by strengthening our inner muscles so that we can hold ourselves steady. That will never work. Imagine yourself on a rowboat, rowing across a choppy ocean, trying to keep yourself traveling in a straight line. The waves keep moving you this way and that way. You think, if only I was stronger then I could keep this boat moving straight ahead. The fact is, in that small boat, with just those two oars, you could never steady yourself no matter how strong you were.

Now imagine a huge ocean liner on the same choppy sea. The waves that were so big in a rowboat are just little licks on the side of the gigantic hull. The ocean liner is able to move completely straight, unaffected by the choppiness that had been so impossible to navigate in the rowboat.

We gain equanimity by increasing the weight of our being, so that we become so spiritually heavy that we are unmoved by the surface fluctuations of life. And the way we increase our spiritual weight is by spending time resting in awakened awareness. Once you find the space of inner freedom and innocence, which is the space of perfect contentment and true equanimity, then you have to spend time resting there so that your spiritual being gains substance. You become more spiritually dense the longer you rest in unbroken contentment. That accumulation of spiritual weight is what allows us to maintain equanimity.

As you sit, allow yourself to find the place in you that has always been the center of your being. The place that has experienced all your experiences. The place that never moves. Find your center and then notice that everything moves around it. It is still. Find that center and rest there in steadiness, stillness, in equanimity.

CHAPTER SEVENTEEN
LET THE POWER OF FAITH
UNLEASH YOUR MEDITATION

Recently I had the chance to spend seven full days, morning until night, on a silent retreat. When it was done, I was disappointed that I hadn't had any major breakthrough experiences. I'd had some insights and revelations and some wonderfully peaceful meditations, but nothing dramatic that felt earth-shattering.

Of course, I know (and teach) that meditation is not about big spiritual experiences. It's about sitting and resting in a stance of radical acceptance of the way things are. But, of course, like everyone else, I like a big spiritual pop when I can get one.

So, for seven days, I sat calmly through each meditation accepting whatever happened.

More often than not, I was just sitting, slightly bored, watching thoughts roll through my head. I felt disappointed at times, and of course there were other times when I was held lovingly in a deep sense of peace and clarity.

The whole time I just did my practice, which means I let it all be exactly what it was without making any problem out of it. I didn't try to work harder. I didn't try to figure anything out - and when I did catch myself working harder or figuring things out, I didn't make a problem out of that either. I just let all that be what it was too.

As the days went on, I found myself drifting in and out of the mediation room, in and out of my practice, in and out of thoughts and feelings.

Drifting without concern. Nothing dramatic but very peaceful and calm. So the retreat ended and, after another week away, I returned home.

When I walked into my house, I realized that I had let go much more than I had realized during the retreat. I walked around and felt like a stranger in my own home. I couldn't relate to anything. The life that I remembered living in this house felt like it belonged to someone else.

I looked at the books on the shelves and I wondered who it was who had bought them. While I was away, a package had arrived with a book in it that I had ordered before the trip. It didn't feel like me who had ordered it.

I kept looking at all the familiar objects in the house and none of them felt like they were related to me anymore.

I was profoundly free of the entanglements of my previous life. It felt like I could just float off into something completely different. It was disconcerting and totally exhilarating at the same time.

It became clear that this is part of the power of just letting things be as they are. Just sitting in silence, stillness and rest for seven days disentangles you from your previous identity and habits of being.

What amazes me about this experience is how much momentum of passive abidance in pure consciousness I had built during the retreat. It happened with no especially dramatic experience; simply by leaning back and resting in the calm abidance of the ever-present original awareness.

The momentum I built during the retreat stayed with me very strongly for a few weeks after returning home and is still with me as I write this some weeks later in a softer form.

As I said earlier, meditation and awakening are not about experiences, they're about what we see as a result of our experiences. So, the question is, what do I see now differently than before this experience? What has this experience revealed to me?

What I want to share with you is my conviction and profound faith in the power of practice.

I've always taught that what you experience in meditation doesn't matter. What matters is doing the practice, and not making a problem out of anything that you experience while you do it. No matter what happens, you just let it rise up and pass away without engaging it at all.

If you do this, you'll break the habit of mental reactivity and build momentum toward calm abidance in the pure consciousness that is always there beyond any particular experience of mind.

I am so passionate about the power of meditation that I feel like I want to shout it louder than ever from every rooftop!

The ultimate source of love and wisdom that we seek, the peace and calm that compels us to practice, our own liberation from unnecessary suffering - is already ours! It is already here! It's not in front of us where we tend to look. It's behind us.

We can't find the source of awareness by turning around because we will still be trying to look at it head on and it will never be an object in front of us that we can see.

We can only find it by leaning back and resting in the consciousness that is always awake, always calm, always present, always wise, always compassionate, and always right there waiting for you to relax into it.

So, when you practice meditation, just allow everything to arise and pass away without making a problem out of any of it and without getting caught up in any effort to make anything other than the way it is. Just do that and let your awakening unfold unimpeded.

Trust that the experiences you have - or don't have - are exactly what you need for this part of the journey. Have faith in the power of practice and let everything else take care of itself.

The true benefit of our spiritual experiences is the faith and confidence they give that allow us to surrender more deeply to our practice.

Spending time resting in the assumption of no problem is the practice that will build a movement of freedom inside you that will liberate your relationship to life.

The freedom you seek is yours - as soon as you stop looking for it and just lean back and rest in it.

And there is still one more thing to share. While the inner freedom that we discover in deep meditation may be the end of seeking, it is also the beginning of a mystical journey that can last a lifetime.

You see depths of detachment are not the true benefit of our practice. The true benefit is the shift in perspective that results from that profound state of inner freedom. From that deeply relaxed awareness, you see things differently. Things that had seemed crucial in your life suddenly don't feel meaningful. Other things that had seemed insignificant suddenly seem critical. From this liberated vantage point you have the chance to consciously choose which aspects of your previous life to reengage with.

You don't have to jump back into your life wholesale, exactly the way it was. You return from such an excursion with a clear sense of what is truly important to your deepest self. You can feel which aspects of your life are aligned with that and which might not be, and you can embrace those that are and let go of those that are not.

And, as you make more conscious choices about how to live, you have more and more intuitions and insights about new possibilities to live into. The mystical journey is a journey of discovery and manifestation in which your life becomes an even clearer reflection of what you recognize to be truly significant.

So, here's the big takeaway.

Yes, spiritual experiences are important! Those moments when we are catapulted beyond our normal perception of reality into vast new vistas of possibility are tremendously inspiring. They feed our passion for liberation and fortify our faith in the ultimate possibility.

At the same time spending time in meditation simply accepting whatever experience we happen to be having is what ultimately liberates our consciousness. It liberates us from our previous habits of identification and makes it possible for us to transform our lives.

What I realized so strongly during the days immediately following this particular retreat is that practicing having no problem in meditation for an extended period of time builds a momentum of freedom inside your-self.

So, the next time you're meditating and not having whatever experience you think you should be having, remember to be totally content with that. Your willingness to be content even in the presence of disappoint-ment is building a momentum of freedom that is liberating your consciousness.

Once your consciousness is free, you can look at your life with new eyes and embrace those aspects that are most aligned with your soul's calling, let go of things that are misaligned, and invite in new possibilities that will move you closer to your spiritual destiny.

PART THREE
REFLECTIONS ON THE SPIRITUAL JOURNEY

In this part of the book, we explore the essence of spiritual life and discover how our lives can be moved and guided by the love, wisdom, and energy of a higher source.

CHAPTER EIGHTEEN
WHAT IS SPIRITUALITY?

Those of us seeking to live lives of deeper meaning, inner peace and lasting freedom have become comfortable with the word spiritual. But, before we get too comfortable with it, let's not assume that we all know what we mean by it, or even if we are all talking about the same thing. So, I want to ask us to consider what it is that we actually mean when we describe something as spiritual.

Try it for yourself. You might find it harder than you imagine to define the word spiritual given how comfortable we've become assuming we already know what it means.

The root of the word spiritual is spirit and the English word spirit comes from Latin roots meaning breath. If you think about your body, breathing appears to be one of the most fundamental ways that we take in the life force energy that sustains us - the energy that animates us and allows us to live, move, think, feel and act.

Spirit then could be seen as the animating energy of life - the life force energy.

So, anything we call spiritual must relate to the energy that animates us, moves us and allows us to live, think, feel and act. If we look into this deeply enough, we begin to realize that we are not separate from this energy. In fact, it is more accurate to say that it is the life force energy itself that lives, thinks, feels and acts, through us.

So, what is it that shapes how the miraculous energy of life shows up through us in the differing ways that it does? What are the cares and concerns, the interests and desires, that make us live, think, feel, and act, the way we do?

To me, spirituality is about opening the flow of life force energy in individuals and in groups of individuals, and then learning how to participate with that flow of energy so that it is allowed to express its full potential in us and manifest in the most beautiful and beneficial ways for everyone.

Spiritual work is whatever practices and studies we use to open to the energy of life and then align with the flow of that energy in more beautiful and beneficial ways.

Meditation has always been an important opening practice for me. The practice of simply sitting and not making a problem out of anything can initiate a process of profound illumination.

You see, we are all deeply conditioned in ways that limit how life's energy can flow through us. There are a multitude of assumed boundaries that govern what we can and cannot do, think, say, and feel.

I often speak about this by pointing out that we live inside a paradigm made up of habitual ways of perceiving and interpreting our experience that limit what we imagine is possible for us - and what we imagine is possible for us becomes the limit of what actually is possible for us. That is how life's energy flow becomes limited by our own assumptions of limitation.

It must also be said that, sometimes, the limitations we take on are valuable because they shape us in ways that are harmonious to life on this planet and allow us to live harmoniously with others within agreed upon structures of society.

However, at some point when we start to feel suffocated by the constraints of cultural assumptions and personal fears, we feel compelled to grow beyond them. We want to heal and expand into greater freedom. We know more is possible and we commit to realizing it. Our spiritual life has begun.

As we begin to move beyond our previous boundaries and limitations, we find that our conditioning starts to work against us. We experience fear as we dare to expand beyond the edges of the dominant paradigm.

As we approach the edge of life as we have known it, our instincts try to drive us back. They warn us of emanate danger in an attempt to convince us that we would be crazy to continue.

Through spiritual practices like meditation, we learn how to be nonreactive to our mind's misguided complaints and develop a degree of presence and composure that allows us to expand into unknown territory.

We might also engage with energetic practices that help liberate our energy from the emotional blocks that bind our heart, mind, and body. I've worked with different forms of yoga, breathwork practices, and the Hawaiian bodywork of Ancient Lomi Lomi and all have proven to be powerful tools for opening and liberating the spirit.

Opening and freeing our energy is critical, but it's not enough on its own.

As our energy opens, we gain access to greater power and creativity and we need to align our energy with spirit to allow it to manifest in beautiful and beneficial ways.

In this part of the book, we will explore the work of spiritual alignment. We will learn how to deeply question some of the foundational assumptions about life and ourselves that create false blocks and limitations. Pursuing these lines of inquiry will lead us into greater clarity about who we really are and what we are actually capable of.

I'm so enthusiastic about the study of philosophy and spiritual ideas because I know how powerful they can be in uprooting the old belief systems and assumptions that are limiting us.

Questions like "Who am I?" "What is the purpose of life?" "Why do I think the way I do?" "Why do I act the way I do?", lead us down a journey of discovery that can radically transform who we are.

I believe a human being is a flow of divine energies and the aim of spiritual work is to open to and align with the flow of divine energy in the most creative, constructive, beautiful and beneficial ways possible.

In this part of the book, we will explore spiritual growth as the work of opening and directing the flow of life that we are.

CHAPTER NINETEEN
THE MIRACLE OF MEDITATION

My first book was called *The Miracle of Meditation* and that title perfectly describes exactly what I feel unendingly inspired to share with people.

My own practice of meditation has blessed me with the experience of a miracle, a miracle so beautiful and life-transforming that I've been tirelessly sharing it with people all over the world nonstop for many years and intend to continue sharing for the rest of my life.

So, what is the miracle of meditation?

Simply put, it is the discovery that life is an unfolding process guided by a universal source of wisdom and love, and the further discovery that the direct recognition of that life source is immediately available to any of us as soon as we stop being distracted by anything else.

As we have already stated, our attention has been limited to a very small range of experience to a much greater degree than any of us ever suspect. What we normally have access to in consciousness is merely a speck in an ocean of possibility.

Our awareness has been caught in a loop like a dog tied to a tree. The small circle defined by the length of our mental chains becomes the limit of our world and life.

The big cosmic joke is that there is no chain binding us. We are penned in by an invisible fence that only exists in our mind. The fence that defines the limits of our life is nothing more than a collection of ideas about who we are and what is possible for us.

When we sit to meditate, we don't do anything. We stop trying to manipulate or control our experience in any way. We simply allow everything to be exactly the way it is.

It took many years of diligent practice before I was able to give up control for even a few moments in meditation. Yet, those few precious moments of freedom were enough to change everything.

117

We tend to assume that when we give up control everything is going to stop, but the truth is that nothing stops. That's part of the miracle because, by seeing that nothing changes, we recognize that we were never in control. It was all just happening and our sense of being in control is just another thing that just keeps happening.

What you discover in these moments of total release is that everything you thought was you was actually a part of an unfolding process of life. Your own self, the seemingly independent choices you make, and all the effort you've expended to get to where you are, was all a naturally arising part of the life process. You were never the one doing it. It was all happening spontaneously and effortlessly.

When this miraculous state of awareness descends upon you, you find that all of the thoughts and feelings that are so familiar just keep happening. Your aspirations and dreams, your fears and concerns, the helpful coaching that you always offer yourself; everything just keeps going. And you realize that all of the voices you used to think were you thinking and talking to yourself were just part of the unfolding habits of mind.

None of those voices were ever you and you suddenly don't know who you are.

Can you see how liberating this is?

All of those voices are just habits running along prescribed paths. The longer you sit in meditation and watch them, the more you see that they just keep going in predictable patterns. You realize you've been trapped in mental loops because you had mistakenly thought they were you.

Now you're a free-floating point of awareness. You see and hear all the thoughts and feelings, but you aren't caught in the belief that they are who you are. You have broken free of the limitation of false identification with thought and feeling.

As I said, even a moment or two of letting go this deeply changes everything.

Some people may protest and want to protect their current sense of free will and choice, but the miracle of meditation doesn't take your freedom away. In fact, it is an exercise of the greatest freedom there is – the freedom to choose to give up control and bring yourself into direct contact with the ever-present movement of the process of life.

Before experiencing the miracle of meditation, we felt like an isolated individual struggling to navigate through the confines of a busy mind. Now, we see ourselves as a mysterious source of awareness floating in an ocean of consciousness that is much bigger than any mind we have ever known.

Everything looks different and the problems we thought we had start to vanish – not because we've solved them, but because our attention is becoming riveted on something else. Something so awe-inspiring that we can't take our eyes off it.

We are captivated by the true nature of life, by the love and wisdom that has always been guiding it, and by the unfathomable reality of who we are.

That is the miracle of meditation.

CHAPTER TWENTY
ENTERING THE MYSTERIES OF THE UNIVERSE

My work is dedicated to facilitating a shift in paradigm that will liberate the divine energy of life to flow freely through our human lives.

The first aspect of what I do, as we explored in the last chapter, involves liberating our consciousness from the constraints of the current paradigm through practices such as meditation. The freedom we win through our spiritual practice liberates our imagination so that we are free to envision dramatically new ways of being.

I sometimes refer to this initial liberation of consciousness as the process of *un-worlding* because we are essentially removing ourselves from the only world we have ever known.

You see, we are worlded. We don't live in reality; we live in a conception of reality - a world. We don't experience things the way they are, we experience things the way we believe they are. We live in a world that is profoundly shaped by our preconceived assumptions about it.

It is possible, either through effort or just dumb luck, to have your consciousness slip out of the grooves that contain it. In these moments, often recognized as profound spiritual experiences, we discover possibilities we never dreamed of.

Suddenly, we know beyond doubt that the world is not necessarily the way it appears to be. Once we have such an experience, it is very difficult to go back to the naivety we once had about reality.

As a meditation teacher, a big part of my job is to create the conditions for people to experience radical leaps in perception. This is a very tricky thing to do.

The challenge arises because it is simultaneously much easier than anyone ever suspects and, at the very same time, so much more dramatic and explosive than we imagine.

It is so hard for us to embrace something that is so simple and yet leads to such dramatic shifts. We either assume that nothing that simple could really work or we make things more complicated than they really are.

In order to be ready for awakening, enlightenment, satori, God-realization, or whatever we want to call it, we have to be prepared for both the ease and the magnitude of the experience.

Awakening is always waiting for us in the consciousness that exists beyond our familiar patterns of thought and feeling. Our thoughts and feelings don't have to go away. We just have to stop paying attention to them.

It is so simple. Anyone can do it for an instant. Try it; just for a moment stop paying attention to anything that you are thinking or feeling.

For that moment your attention falls into, well nowhere, and focuses on nothing.

It gets difficult when you try to leave your attention in that empty place for longer than just a moment or two. It feels like nothing. How can we pay attention to nothing? What do we focus on if there is nothing there?

We are so deeply conditioned to focus on something that it feels impossible to focus on nothing at all.

We are addicted to paying attention to specific thoughts and feelings that arise in consciousness. We have certain set patterns of mind that we feel at home with and everything else feels like it doesn't even exist. There is simply nothing there to pay attention to.

If we learn how to rest in the uncertainty of having no particular thoughts or feelings to pay attention to, something will begin to dawn on us. We will see that when we stop looking at the inner objects of the mind, the world disappears and we disappear with it.

Ultimately, this is what is so frightening and why true awakening will probably always remain a rare attainment. When the part of us that we always thought was all of us starts to disappear we panic. In the face of non-existence, our attention snaps back to the familiar. It shifts focus back onto something it knows.

The deepening of practice involves increasing our ability to rest unflinchingly in the unknown. When we find the courage and the strength to rest in the unknown, a process of transformation is initiated. The first step of the process is the dissolution of the self and the world. It is the disappearance of everything.

The second part of the process is the discovery of the previously invisible worlds that have always existed beyond the thoughts and feelings that have been consuming our attention. When we discover these, they seem both utterly foreign and deeply familiar.

You see, there is always a part of us that has been aware of the invisible energies beyond the familiar mind. We have always been aware of the deeper levels of our being. So, when we consciously return to these subtle perceptions, it is really a reunion with a deeper part of ourselves.

We have come home to ourselves and we are seeing again what we always knew was there. Everything is the way it always was and yet everything is completely different.

When I teach meditation, I try very hard not to speak about it in a way that will make it feel like some kind of long laborious path to somewhere very far from where you already are. Instead, it is a simple shift in perception more like turning your head to see what is on your left when you have spent a lifetime looking right.

The danger of teaching this way is that people might think that there is nothing to it. That awakening isn't that different from their normal perception of the world. Nothing could be further from the truth. In trying to convey the closer than close quality of awakening, you can inadvertently encourage people to settle for far less than what is possible.

Awakening changes everything even if everything stays exactly the same. I know meditation is the simplest thing you can possibly do, but it is also the most difficult. Embracing the practice in a life-altering way will take everything you have. But it's worth it!

125

We are so much more than we think we are. It is time for us to embrace all of who we are and allow a very different form of living to emerge on this planet.

Your consciousness is the consciousness of the entire cosmos. Your life is part of the living edge of a cosmic being that is constantly stretching and reaching into further possibilities. We are that cosmic being. And that cosmic being manifests as an unimaginable singular whole being and, at the same time, as the pristine uniqueness of each and every individual form of it.

It doesn't matter what we think we have or have not experienced so far.

No one is disqualified from this adventure. All are welcome.

Whatever we have experienced is only meaningful when it allows us to have greater access to the inconceivable mystery of being. In the face of the unknowable, we are all newborns forever.

Those of us who think we have not had enough experience can mistakenly slip into the belief that we need some kind of experience before we can wake up. Those of us who have had many spiritual experiences can easily slip into the belief that we already know everything.

Every moment is an opportunity to let everything go. It is a perfect chance to enter existence completely fresh, without any ideas about ourselves.

When you sit to meditate, just place your attention on the inconceivable part of consciousness beyond the familiar mind and leave it there. Allow the mysteries of being to reveal themselves before your very eyes. Allow a process of transformation to take you to places you never dreamed of before.

CHAPTER TWENTY-ONE
BECOMING AVAILABLE FOR
WHAT'S NEXT

My life, since the age of 29, has been consciously dedicated to the pursuit of spiritual growth and awakening. For over a quarter of a decade, every other aspect of life has been secondary to my spiritual work and vision.

This depth of focus and devotion has blessed me with miraculous experiences of awakening and an orientation to the spiritual path that recognizes the value of deep surrender.

Any of us who have decided to share our spiritual experience publicly have come to our insight and understanding in different ways. For some, sudden, seemingly unsought for, explosions of grace initiated them to the path of teaching. For others, extreme suffering catalyzed the release of spirit from which they teach.

In my own case, whatever spiritual riches I have to share came to me by way of hard and devoted spiritual work and practice.

For two decades, I lived in a residential practice community where I did hundreds of thousands of hours of spiritual practice and study. As I look back on it now, I see that my real practice was being perpetually available for whatever was next. All of the meditation, chanting, prostrations and study supported me to be available, but being available was the primary practice.

All of those years of practice have brought me to the conclusion that the ultimate spiritual practice is living surrender. That means being perpetually available for spirit's next call.

Most of us are not available. We are busy. Busy with our lives, busy with our problems, busy with all of the things that make up our lives. We may be listening for the call of spirit, but we are often listening through ears that are clouded by their own considerations.

The divine could be offering opportunities for dramatic awakening ten or a hundred times a day and we are simply not available to notice.

There are layers and layers and layers of stuff that we can be busy with. And of course, our pursuit of spiritual practice can be something we are very very busy with too. If we are busy with our practice, we are just as unavailable as if we were busy making money. Busy is busy.

Being available means not being busy with anything. It means being done with everything.

Nothing you do, gain or accomplish will ever be enough. In the end, you just have to decide to be done. To stop seeking, to stop looking and be available for whatever is next. That is when the real spiritual life begins.

In my case, all of that extreme practice did seem to help me let go, give up, and stop seeking for more.

I believe it's possible to create conditions that give you the opportunity to do practice and live in perpetual availability at least for a time. I believe that opportunities for radical spiritual practice can be created and I believe that intensive practice needs to be engaged with cautiously within a protective environment. What makes spiritual practice safe is surrounding it with a spirit of love and good will.

So, how do we engage with intensive practice safely without the practice losing its potency?

First of all, your practice must be inspired and not forced. You must be presented with a possibility that you find so compelling that it calls you to go places you never imagined you could. You should not be pushed into awakening from behind, but guided from the front. This allows your spiritual unfolding to happen organically in alignment with your own needs, desires and capacities.

Secondly, the circumstances in which the practice is happening must be stable and free of drama. This means both the immediate surroundings during practice as well as your life in general. Intense practice is destabilizing enough. There is no reason to add additional risk by practicing without the proper support. Don't manufacture intensity by disrupting your life unnecessarily. If the circumstances of your life need to change it will be obvious; if it's not obvious don't force it.

In the end, the big event is not an experience that you are going to have in practice. It is the recognition that you don't need any more experiences. Some people recognize that they don't need any more experiences after having very few. Others, like me, seemed to have needed a lot of them before we were ready to let go. The end result is the same. We stop seeking and let go.

Since dramatic spiritual breakthroughs are not ultimately the point, I suggest you do enough practice to have the experiences you need as quickly as possible so you are available for what's next.

Are you ready to be done with the path and be truly available for life?

CHAPTER TWENTY-TWO
AWAKENING AND ENLIGHTENMENT

When we talk about the spiritual path, we use the words awakening and enlightenment as metaphors to explain profound shifts in our experience. In this chapter, I'll offer one way to understand the difference.

The most common use of the word awakening describes what happens to us each morning – we wake up. One of the ways we can think about what it means to wake up from sleep is that we return to direct contact with who and where we already are.

When we are asleep, we dream. Maybe we dream we are a captain of a ship, or a child in school, or a damsel in the middle ages. When we wake up and we find ourselves lying in bed exactly where we were before we fell asleep, we remember who we are in the real world or in our waking life.

Extending this analogy to spiritual awakening, we would say that the life that we are living right now is a dream. The you that is reading these words is a dream version of you. It is not who you really are. The me that I feel myself to be as I type these words is also a dream self.

It is important to remember that the person in the dream is not the one that is going to wake up, just like the ship captain in the dream did not wake up to find that he or she was really asleep in bed. The ship captain was real in the dream but isn't there in bed in the morning once we wake up.

I use the word awakening, in the spiritual sense, to describe events that leave us knowing that we are ultimately not the person who responds to our name and has our history. We are more than that and life is much bigger and more magical than we had imagined.

When I use the word enlightenment (which I seldom do), I want to imply something more significant than awakening because it has to do with our ongoing level of connection to the truth of who we really are and how fully that truth is reflected in our daily lives.

Awakening implies having had an experience of who we really are. En-lightenment implies having an ongoing connection with the reality of who we really are and living as that. You could say that awakening is digital and enlightenment is analog.

We are either awake or not awake. We either know that we are more than we think we are or we don't. We have either glimpsed the wider reality beyond what we can see or we haven't. It's one or the other. And if you are reading this book then I am asserting you must be awake. Otherwise, this would not be interesting to you at all.

Enlightenment, on the other hand, is not an either/or. It is an ongoing process of deepening recognition and embodiment of the truth of who we really are. As we surrender to the reality that has been revealed to us, that knowing becomes consistently available to us in a mysterious way and our life becomes an expression of it.

Functionally, that means we cannot be fooled by the experience of the dream self any more - even if it continues to be our experience much, if not most, of the time. We know who we are even when we're experiencing ourselves through the dream of the separate self.

Even when our conscious experience is of our separate self – the one who was born on our birthday, has our history and responds to our name – we still maintain some mysterious knowing of who we really are. It is not something we can look at and see directly, and yet we can feel it just beyond the edge of our conscious experience.

Both the awakened individual and the enlightened individual continue to have periodic and often dramatic experiences of who they really are. The difference is that the awakened person needs these experiences in order to have faith in the truth of who they really are. The enlightened person is certain about who they are without needing any more experiences to prove it.

The journey into deeper enlightenment is the journey into deeper faith and confidence in the truth of who we are. This deep spiritual confidence gives us greater and greater access to the mysterious knowing of our infinite Self. If you meet a deeply enlightened person, they seem to live always half in this world and half in direct contact with the mystery beyond it.

As a person deepens into enlightened recognition, they also become a more and more consistent expression of the divine union that lies behind the illusion of separation. That divine union is the union that occurs as we return to direct contact with who we really are.

The way we've been trained to think is that we start out as a baby born in a body and then we gradually learn about who we are. We learn that we are a human person, that we have unique characteristics, that we have a history and a future, and eventually we will die and leave this body, or perhaps just end.

By the time we reach adulthood, we are more or less completely convinced that we are the person who has our name, was born on our birthday, abides wholly within our body, and will die at some as yet undisclosed moment in the future.

The moment of awakening occurs when we realize, through some experience or other, that we are more than that.

Enlightenment means having, to some degree or other, ongoing, trans-experiential, direct access to the mysterious and inconceivable truth of who we are.

The experience of enlightenment is a barely visible ongoing sense that we extend infinitely beyond the edges of our perception. We live our life, engaging with ourselves and the world as they are seen through our minds and yet knowing the whole time that it is all just a tiny slice of a vast unimaginable wholeness.

How did we do it in the first place? How did an infinite being cram itself into the tiny space of a single human life?

We do it by being taught to believe that we are a separate self and then developing a relentless habit of tracking that self constantly through time and space.

At the moment of birth, the timeless and un-locate-able awareness that is the consciousness of reality gets focused into and through the perceptual apparatus of a newly born biological entity on the surface of planet Earth. This awareness is quickly engaged by other entities of the species that calls itself human.

The baby is brought into an unlearning process in which it soon forgets its Self. It is introduced to the idea that it just appeared out of nowhere. It soon forgets where it was before. It eventually disconnects from conscious awareness of its own source and becomes convinced that it began with the emergence of this body and is limited to this one single lifetime.

The process of awakening and enlightenment is a re-learning of who we truly are. We don't re-learn ourselves by reading about who we are in books. That is just a way for the separate self to gain knowledge about another person's experience of who they really are.

The re-learning process occurs through a profound effort of breaking the habits of locating ourselves in time and space. If we can stop tracking ourselves, if we can lose our sense of who we are as a separate being that exists in a specific location at a specific time, then we naturally land in the truth of who we are.

It is possible through spiritual practice to stop insisting that we are only this or only that, that we are only here and not there, and that we exist only now and not then. If we have the courage to stop keeping track of ourselves, to let go of any sense of limitation, and to lose our sense of self completely, we will make a shocking discovery.

We are everything, always, everywhere! That is the discovery of who we really are as an inseparable infinite and eternal wholeness. Making this shocking discovery for ourselves is the great opportunity of spiritual practice and of the mystical journey.

Awakening occurs when we glimpse the truth of who we are for long enough to leave us divinely confused about who we are.

Enlightenment is the state of being convinced that we are an incomprehensible, infinite and eternal wholeness. As we become more and more convinced, our connection to the truth of who we are will become unshakeable so that, no matter how much the sense of separation may dominate our experience at any given moment, somewhere in the mysterious depths of our being we always know who we are and, inevitably, the life that we live will become a more and more perfect expression of that wholeness.

CHAPTER TWENTY-THREE
THE FIRST AND SECOND
SURRENDERS OF MEDITATION

In this chapter, we will name a distinction that I sometimes speak of as the first and second surrender of spiritual meditation and that has already been spoken about in earlier chapters without naming it as such.

The first surrender of meditation is the utterly passive acceptance of everything that is.

The meditation that I teach is called The Practice of No Problem and it allows us to rest in a pristine space of profound contentment where nothing whatsoever is wrong. Some of us have spent hours resting in that state of mind where everything is perfect as it is. It is a heaven of peaceful abidance in which you don't need anything more than what is already present; there is nothing to do and nowhere to be but here.

As we rest in this perfect place – in practice or in life – something mysterious, miraculous and magical begins to happen. We start to realize that the emptiness we are abiding in is not empty. The space in which we find ourselves is an ocean of consciousness in which currents of awakening constantly move and swirl, opening into possibilities that can become the journey of a lifetime.

Our perception of these currents starts as subtle stirrings – little whispers of guidance and insight. It is like hearing a faint sound in the distance, a barely noticeable scent in the air, or an impossibly faint brush against our skin. As the currents of awakening pass though us, they stir our soul into a deeper recognition of itself and its potential. These stirrings invite us into the miracle of perpetual awakening.

The second surrender of meditation involves allowing yourself to be captured by the currents of awakening and carried off into the mystical adventure they invite us to.

This second movement of surrender is subtle. It involves a choice, but it's not an activity of the will. You are not doing something; you are allowing something that has already begun to continue.

Earlier I spoke about how meditation is like falling in love, and thinking about meditation in this way can really help illuminate what the second surrender of meditation is.

As I already described, the moment when you realize that you are falling in love is magic. In that moment, a choice needs to be made. You need to decide to allow the process of falling in love to continue, or to stop it. This isn't a choice between doing one thing or doing something else. It is a choice between allowing something that is already happening to continue or to make the effort required to stop it. It is a choice between passively allowing ourselves to be moved or effortfully stopping a movement that is already in process.

The same is true of spiritual love. There is a moment when you feel your feet start to leave the ground, your head gets a little dizzy, or lighthearted bubbles of joy start to float through your body. You realize that you're being carried away. You are falling in love – not with a person – but with a spiritual destiny. The doorway to divine adventure has opened and a mysterious attractive force is pulling you toward it.

Whether we are talking about romantic love or spiritual love, the critical question remains the same - will you allow yourself to be taken? Are you available for a dance of spiritual unfolding? Or will you stand rigidly in place?

I sometimes refer to the first surrender of meditation in terms of the attainment of spiritual freedom and the second surrender as the journey of creative illumination. Both are essential as part of the path of awakening and enlightenment.

The first surrender is essential because it is what liberates our awareness from our habitual patterns of mind. If we let ourselves be carried by inner impulses before we have liberated our awareness from its habitual patterns, we will ultimately repeat them.

The second surrender is what makes us available to experience and ultimately realize new possibilities. If we do not surrender to the subtle currents of spirit once we recognize them, we can get stuck in a detached witnessing position that becomes dull and even indifferent.

144

CHAPTER TWENTY-FOUR
FLOW STATES AND HIGHER WAYS OF BEING

We are self-aware. We don't just experience the world, we experience ourselves experiencing it.

Spiritual liberation is often spoken about as the attainment of Self-Awareness, but I think it might be better understood as the loss of self-awareness.

Over the past few hundred years, particularly in Western culture, humanity has been very busy developing a strong and stable sense of self.

We've built up a powerful cultural capacity to hold an abstract image of ourselves and use it as an ever-present reference point.

We've become so deeply identified with our sense of self that we tend to equate consciousness with self-awareness and so self-aware consciousness is the only form of consciousness we recognize. That means that if we don't see evidence that something is aware of itself like we are, we tend to think of it as unconscious.

Even in relation to ourselves, we will describe ourselves as unconscious when we're aware of something but don't know that we're aware of it. Since we don't recognize awareness unless we are aware of being aware, we relate to unselfconscious awareness as no awareness at all.

This is the biggest spiritual challenge to overcome on the path to spiritual liberation.

The spiritual liberation we seek is the loss of self-awareness. It means letting go of the part of you that experiences yourself experiencing and just becoming absorbed in the direct experience of life.

But because we define awareness only in terms of self-awareness, we will not be satisfied with a liberation that we cannot see. We don't want to be free. We want to experience ourselves being free.

As soon as you let go of the need to know that you're free, you will discover that you already are. You are already having a direct, immediate, unmitigated experience of reality. At some level, you are already free of your self-image and its distorting influence on your perception. You just don't recognize that awareness because it isn't an awareness that you can see yourself having.

This insight, if you let it have you and let it flip everything inside out, will radically change everything without anything at all needing to change.

It will be worth taking a little time to explore the implications of giving up our self-centered view of consciousness.

The part of us that is aware of being aware is our self-conscious sense of self. When we define consciousness exclusively in terms of self-consciousness then consciousness becomes the exclusive property of the sense of self. Consciousness, we wrongly assume, belongs to the ego rather than to existence. The consciousness of existence has become trapped inside our self-image.

Spiritual liberation is the liberation of consciousness from its current bondage to the human sense of self.

The promise of spiritual liberation is that the profound creative potential that human beings have been developing will finally be at the service of existence itself.

When we get our sense of self out of the way, the concerns of existence will move us. Our incredible self-aware consciousness will not disappear, it will simply become available for a universal being.

The biggest reason to pursue spiritual liberation is so the true creative potential of the human spirit can be available to serve universal concerns.

In pursuing spiritual freedom, it is helpful to see it as a kind of flow state because, in flow states, life just occurs. Many of us have experienced the exhilarating experience of being in flow. Flow occurs when we do things but we are not aware of doing them. We don't feel like we are doing them. Everything is just happening.

When I write, I often get into a flow where I find that I've written for an hour and can't remember what I wrote. I often go back and read it and think, "Wow, this is really good." As if I am reading it myself for the first time.

I also paint, and sometimes my brush just flows over the canvas and amazing shapes and colors appear in front of my eyes. I was not planning any of it and, once they appear, I don't know where they came from.

And finally, when I give an Ancient Lomi Lomi massage, there are times when my touch is not guided by my mind. It is guided by the sensation of the skin alone. I have no thoughts about what I'm doing. I am simply in service of a massage that wants to happen.

The primary characteristic of flow is that you forget yourself. You get so into what you're doing that you forget about yourself doing it. You lose self-awareness. When this happens, you feel so free!

Spiritual liberation is a special kind of flow state because it occurs when we're not doing anything at all.

In normal flow states, we get absorbed in a particular activity. It could be skateboarding, knitting, dancing, or tennis, but in most flow states there is something that captivates our attention long enough to allow us to forget ourselves.

The experience of spiritual liberation is a state of flow that involves only being. Meditation is a practice that is ripe for igniting these liberating flow states.

If we sit in meditation and allow ourselves to get absorbed in the experience of being, all of our attention will be consumed by the miracle of awareness itself. You forget about yourself. You are just absorbed in being aware. You forget about what you are absorbed in. There is just awareness.

If you have time to rest in the inherent amazement of being, you start to forget how you used to watch yourself. You are just absorbed in being.

If you are lucky enough to be on retreat when this occurs, you may have the luxury of continuing to let go even when you're not meditating. You find yourself walking around between sessions not sure of who you are and not knowing who is doing anything.

In this open state of mind, you are profoundly available to be moved by the love and wisdom of existence itself. You've stopped directing life and you're ready for a greater insight, intuition and care to move you forward.

Your separate sense of self is no longer the one seeing through your eyes, feeling your emotions, or generating the wisdom that continually arises in your mind.

The spiritual liberation we seek is not our own. Without realizing, it we have always been seeking the liberation of the higher possibility that exists within us.

There is a new way of being that is waiting to be born and our spiritual liberation begins the process of setting it free.

CHAPTER TWENTY-FIVE
KUNDALINI AND INNER SPIRITUAL GUIDANCE

Spiritual paths, both traditional and alternative, in one way or another, always involve a call for surrender. Surrender means giving up, letting go, ceasing to resist. The moment of surrender is the moment of initiation. It is the beginning of the journey, not the end. It is a leap of faith that propels us into mystery and adventure.

The moment of surrender often involves a profound and sometimes dramatic healing from the deeply conditioned habit of mistrust and self-protection that most of us have developed. A doorway opens when we find access to a source of deep spiritual wisdom that we know we can trust. That doorway invites us to a new life, but it does not stay open indefinitely. If we hesitate too long, we miss the opportunity and must wait for it to open again.

Spiritual practices are designed to coax the door open. Stepping through the door is the surrender that begins the spiritual life. If we long to awaken and transform, it is important that we are ready to let go when the door opens. We do not need to do anything to pass through the door. We will naturally pass the threshold once it opens as long as we do not resist.

The reason that surrender holds such a central place in spiritual work is because the essence of transformation is a shift in identity from a limited sense of self to an unbounded experience of being. We begin our spiritual search rooted in a culturally inherited identity that I sometimes call the 'thinking-thing.'

We experience ourselves to be isolated individual entities living in a universe that is fundamentally separate from us. We appear to have access to a capacity for conscious awareness that originates inside of us. We use powers of perception and reason to take in information about the world and make decisions in response to it.

In short, we see ourselves as independent agents of activity – beings that make choices and take actions based on internal considerations. This leads to a deep assumption of autonomous control over our lives and the world around us. If you don't think you have such an assumption, look at your internal response when you encounter something that is beyond your control. We feel that we should be masters of our own destiny and we resist outside authority over our lives.

Most spiritual paths are based in the direct recognition that this view is profoundly distorted by a false assumption of separation. In mystical revelation, we recognize that we are not separate from each other, the world, or anything else. All is One, and I am That, has been the declaration of great spiritual realizers of all ages.

When spiritual paths call for surrender, they are asking us to give up our identification with an isolated and separate small 's' self so that we can expand into the fullness of who we are.

As I said earlier, I see surrender as occurring in two stages - whether it comes as the result of specific spiritual practices, spontaneous revelation, or as an unanticipated accident of circumstance.

The first stage is a deep passive acceptance of what is. In that state of abandon, we are available for awakening and ready to pass through the open doorway.

This initial readiness has to be in the form of a passive surrender because we are giving up our current self to become something new. The limited self that we are at the start cannot will itself to be different. Any act of will that originates from the separate sense of self will only serve to reinforce that sense of self. The only way to invite spiritual transformation is to surrender. There may be many things that we do to prepare ourselves for the moment of surrender but, when that moment comes, we have to be ready to be taken.

The uncertainty that we experience when our identity begins to slip away can be terrifying and, if we are not certain that we want to transform, we will find a way to stop it by reasserting our sense of self. Most often, we do this by focusing on the experience that we are having. Once we recognize ourselves to be the-one-who-is-experiencing, we know who we are again and the process of self-forgetting ceases.

If instead we allow ourselves to be swept away, we will lose all sense of who we are and become aware of subtle spiritual energies and sensitivities. These energies are known as Kundalini in the East and, as I experience it, they flow naturally in the direction of optimal spiritual growth. The second stage of surrender is to allow these subtle energies of awakening to guide us along our unique spiritual journey.

In my own meditation practice, I simply sit with the intention 'to have no problem.' No matter what arises in consciousness, I simply allow it and embrace it exactly as it is. I rest in a prior assumption of perfect contentment. Often my mind is roaring and complaining as loudly as ever. I simply don't make a problem out of it. I might see myself acting as if there was a problem, but I don't make a problem out of that either.

My practice is to sit and be perfectly content with my mind no matter how noisy it is. I am ready to sit in the company of my busy mind forever. I am free – free from the need for anything to be other than it is. I sit in complete recognition that the experience I am having, no matter what it is, is enough – completely, gloriously, fully enough.

By resting in this deliberate state of perfect resolution, I have done all that I can. The rest is not up to me. Sometimes an hour or more will go by and nothing will change. My mind keeps racing, but I am fine. I am ready for a miracle, but I am not forcing it or insisting on it. I am simply available for it. This is what meditation is to me.

Sometimes, my mind will slow down and become deeply relaxed and satisfied. In this state, my thoughts and feelings drift away and I find myself floating in empty space with the chatter of my mind a mere distant whisper.

This peaceful state might continue for a long time and I am perfectly happy with this, but no happier than I am with my busy mind. My contentment does not depend on any particular state. I am happy with the way things are no matter how they are.

Sometimes, in this restful place, energy begins to stir. It might be a bodily sensation, or a burst of sound or light. At other times it is an insight, vision or intuition. These stirrings have a distinctive quality. They feel like they are coming from the depths of my being and the heart of the universe. They are gentle but unyielding.

I see these as the energies of awakening aroused from slumber. When they arise, I don't do anything with them. I don't try to encourage or discourage them. I don't hold on or let go. I don't try to remember them or ignore them. I simply remain present and available.

In a wonderful way, the energy starts to move me. I have sometimes felt that it was reorganizing my cellular structure, or rewiring my nervous system. I have endured times of tremendous pain, heart opening bliss, and existential fear. Through it all, I simply practice having no problem.

I meditated for the first time about thirty years ago. It has been a long and varied journey of awakening ever since and the energies of awakening have guided me throughout. First, they supported me to leave my first career as an engineer to give myself unconditionally to spiritual pursuit. Then, they encouraged me to leave my second career as an educator and spend twenty years in an experimental spiritual community until I was guided to leave that behind as well. I have been directed into practices, retreats, insights, revelations, and relationships. This guidance has appeared to me in many forms. I have followed it imperfectly, but well enough to be brought into a life beyond my wildest dreams.

I want you to know that the subtle energy of awakening sometimes called Kundalini is real. It is a living spiritual intelligence and it is available to guide you forward if you have the courage to follow.

CHAPTER TWENTY-SIX
THE EXPANSION OF IMAGINATION

In my opinion what most limits us and keeps us from realizing our highest potentials is not a lack of will, strength, intelligence, or desire. What truly holds us back is a lack of imagination and too often we can't embrace an awakening that has already started because we can't believe it's actually happening to us.

The great gift of spiritual work is the expansion of imagination. What we ultimately gain from the hours we spend in spiritual practice is the ability to imagine possibilities that were simply inconceivable to us before.

I've spent the vast majority of my adult life pursuing awakening. I've spent thousands upon thousands of hours in various forms of spiritual practice. For most of that time I was hoping to have a spiritual experience so dramatically powerful that it would alter my perception of reality forever.

And I did have many powerful awakening experiences but, in the end, I realized that my dream of having one that would stick was not the point. The real value of a spiritual breakthrough is not in the experience itself. It is in how the experience expands your imagination - because once your imagination is stretched into new possibilities, it never fully returns to its original limits.

Possibility is a powerful word. When we say something is possible, it means it can happen. And reality is defined by what is possible and what is not possible. Changing reality means changing what is possible.

Our sense of self is created out of the ideas that we hold about who we are along with the feeling sense that we have of being 'me'. The ideas we hold about ourselves and the way we feel combine to form our identity and our identity plays a central role in defining what is possible for us.

Over a lifetime, the image we hold of ourselves solidifies and creates a stubborn sense of inflexibly restricted possibility. We experience ourselves to be a person for whom some things are possible and others are not. The sense of self is the boundary that defines the range of possibility that we have access to.

There are many spiritual practices that allow you to experience beyond the boundaries of your limited sense of self. The practice of meditation, at least as I learned it, is one of those.

We all have a sense of what reality is. We can imagine the physical universe out to its farthest edges and we have a sense of the inner universe of our minds. The totality of what we imagine we can experience, inside and outside, feels to us like the totality of existence. It feels like all there is.

In our deep spiritual experiences, we open up for a moment or two, or a week, or a month, or longer, to the wider existence of Reality. In those moments, we realize that our normal experience, the one we generally considered to be all that there is, is only a tiny part of a much bigger picture. Spiritual experiences are so liberating because they free us from the narrow confines of our current experience of reality.

Our spiritual experiences open us to unlimited possibility because, in the wake of these experiences, we realize that more is possible than we can imagine. This doesn't mean that everything is possible. It means that we don't know what's possible, and so anything might be.

I want to share with you a term that I read about in a book by a spiritual teacher named E. J. Gold. The term is *maze brightness* and it was used in research involving laboratory rats that were being made to search for food in mazes. The rats were timed to see how long it would take them to find the cheese. Between each trial, the scientists would move the walls of the maze around, before putting the rats back in and repeating the experiment. I imagine these tests were used to see if rats could learn how to navigate a maze more quickly.

One of the most interesting things that was discovered in these tests was that, in a small percentage of cases, a rat would struggle through the maze several times hunting for cheese until something unusual happened - the rat seemed to realize it was in a maze. It suddenly stopped being interested in the cheese. Its eyes widened, its heart rate increased and, from that point on, it was only interested in getting out of the maze. It would no longer travel through the maze looking for cheese, it would only try over and over again to climb up the walls and get out. Somehow, in a sudden flash of illumination, the rat realized that it was trapped.

When we realize that reality as we experience it is a small part of a much wider reality, we have our own version of maze brightness. We call it a spiritual awakening. We realize that we are trapped in a limited sense of ourselves and, from that point forward, we become very interested in expanding into the fullness of who we really are. That is what I see as the whole point of spiritual life. It is all about liberating ourselves from a limited experience into the fullness of reality.

Our mind acts like a filter that takes in information and shapes it into a picture of the way things are. We often forget that our picture of reality has already been shaped and filtered before we are even aware of it. Some information is allowed to flow into our perception, some is not. The information that passes the filter is shaped and organized into particular arrangements that guarantee that we experience reality in certain ways and not others. We are not seeing reality as it is. We are seeing reality as our minds allow us to.

Meditation allows us to relax the mind's filtering mechanisms so we can see beyond them. The deeper you go into meditation, the more you experience reality in a way you never have before.

Meditation becomes the human equivalent of climbing the wall to get out of the maze. We are searching for a way up and out of the mind so that we can see the wider reality beyond it.

One of the most active filtering mechanisms of the mind is the sense of self that we identify with. If I see myself only as Jeff, then I live inside of Jeff's perspectives and Jeff's limited range of possibility. There are certain things that are possible for Jeff, and certain things that are not. The sense of self dictates the range of possibility that we live in. When we experience a wider reality, we see that the sense of being an isolated individual is creating a picture of reality that is not the limit of what is possible.

Meditation is one way for us to let go of the limitations of the mind so we can get a wider view of reality. The time we spend in meditation is an end in itself - and a gateway to more. It is a process of letting go of what is, so that we can become available for new possibilities. The ultimate goal of our practice is to allow a new and larger sense of self to emerge within us that can expand the possibilities of reality. If you hold this context for meditation, your practice will be fueled by a very powerful energy source.

Many people meditate in order to liberate themselves from feelings of pain or suffocation but, when you really start to see the possibilities that meditation opens up and realize that, by letting go of your current experience of reality, you can expand in ways that were previously unimaginable to you, your inspiration increases ten-fold. Your meditation is not just about alleviating discomfort. Now, it has unimaginable creative potential. When I teach meditation, I am really teaching people how to gain access to unlimited creative potential at the level of selfhood.

When you meditate, simply sit and have no problem. Be with whatever your experience is without preference. You might be having the most amazing, peaceful, blissful, easeful experience, or you may be having the most frustrating and uncomfortable experience.

The practice is simply not to make a problem out of it. The beautiful experience and the frustrating experience are exactly equal. Neither is preferable to the other. And if you notice an experience of preference arising, wanting your experience to be one way versus another, don't have a problem with that either. You don't even need to have a preference for having no preference.

Whatever your experience is, allow it to be. This is the simple instruction that opens the door to unlimited possibility.

When you have no preference, the thoughts and feelings of your mind are free to come and go as they please. Positive experiences come. Wonderful insights emerge. Painful or frustrating experiences come.

Sometimes self-doubt or fear emerges. Just let it all come and go. Do nothing to either prolong or stop anything. No preference means allowing the comings and goings of mind to happen as they will. As you do this, you are learning to be content no matter what your mind is experiencing. This is the conscious practice of perfect contentment.

It takes tremendous courage to be content. There is so much momentum behind the belief that we can only be content under certain specific conditions, and we spend so much energy, consciously and unconsciously, trying to create and maintain those conditions. In meditation, we let go of all conditions and allow ourselves to simply be content with exactly the way things are, no matter how they are.

The only reason we ever feel discontent is because we are holding on to an image of the way things should be that doesn't match the way things are. The gap between the way we imagine things should be and the way they are is the source of existential tension. Do you, in this moment, have the courage to be content with the way things are?

If we do not find a way to be content with the way things are, we will never give up control. We will continue our relentless attempts to manipulate and shape our experience. Unfortunately, the one who is doing all the manipulating is the very same limited sense of self that is causing all the discontent in the first place. No matter how it attempts to alter or improve reality, the sense of self remains locked in its limitations and those limitations continue to define what's possible.

If we find a way to be perfectly content with the way things are, something miraculous happens. A new source of energy appears. This energy is not driven by a sense that there is something wrong. It is not motivated by a feeling that things are not the way they should be. The energy of awakening is fueled by a sense of limitless possibility. It always expands into more.

When you embrace the way things are, exactly as they are, you simultaneously allow the energy of possibility to move through you. As a result, your life changes in unimaginable ways because you are no longer simply striving to fix what is wrong and overcome limitation. You are now driven by possibilities that constantly invite you to realize them.

CHAPTER TWENTY-SEVEN
CONSCIOUSNESS IS ALL THERE IS

I entered onto the spiritual path in earnest at a time when the profound esoteric wisdom of the East was being pursued earnestly in many circles. Some of us decided to pursue awakening and enlightenment with single pointed dedication. We lived in communities, did extreme amounts of practices, traveled to India, spent time with teachers and read sacred texts.

The work that I do is deeply inspired by the radical spirit of discovery that was embodied in the mystical traditions of the East and, in this chapter, I want to express the realization of Oneness as I have come to know it.

My spiritual training occurred within the Hindu tradition of Advaita Vedanta and, specifically, in the lineage of the great Indian sage Ramana Maharshi. The goal of this revered spiritual tradition is the experience of non-duality and, ultimately, the surrender of our lives to the wisdom and love inherent in that primordial source of awareness.

It is important to understand that the cultural assumptions about the nature of reality that underlie the tradition of Advaita Vedanta are, in at least one critical way, diametrically opposed to the assumptions about reality that we have been taught in the west.

In the modern West, we live in a materialistic culture. As materialists, we are taught to believe that: the universe is fundamentally a physical space filled with planets and stars; in which at least one planet life formed; at least one species of life consciousness emerged.

The Eastern culture out of which Advaita Vedanta was created is an Idealistic culture. An Idealist is taught to believe that, before there was any universe at all - that means before time, space, matter, or energy - there was pure consciousness. All of what we know as the universe, and everything in it, was created like a dream out of the pure consciousness that started it all.

The experience of non-duality that is central to the goal of Advaita Vedanta is an experience of that original source of pure consciousness and the recognition that "I am That."

Spiritual liberation, as we have been saying thoughout this book, is freedom from the assumed limitations of the small self into the direct recognition of the self absolute or big self. Behind all of our ideas about ourselves and the identity that we hold, we discover that there is nothing but pure consciousness and that initiating source of awareness is the big self that we all really are.

Because we live in a deeply materialistic age, our belief in our own physical existence seems so unquestionable that it is all but impossible to break the spell of solidity that we live under. If we do find a way to let go of the assumption of being a physical entity, we just might stumble upon a direct recognition of our true nature as the free-floating awareness that is the source of everything.

Because our language is built on the assumption of being a separate physical entity, it doesn't lend itself well to communicating non-dual reality. Even using the descriptor free-floating is problematic because it implies the existence of some medium that awareness floats in. That would imply the existence of two; awareness and the medium it floats in. There is no space that awareness floats in. Awareness doesn't exist in space. Awareness just is.

Non-duality is the recognition of oneness without a second. It is the direct realization that conscious awareness is all there is; not a conscious awareness that exists in the universe because the universe itself is only emerging as part of the dream of that one pure consciousness.

Take a moment to consider the possibility that everything we experience, including ourselves, is part of a dream of reality that is generated out of pure consciousness. This statement may not seem shocking to you. Perhaps you've heard similar things before and find it easy to understand and accept, but remember, understanding and accepting is not the same as experiencing. The ultimate prize is being swept up in the direct recognition of our own non-existence as a separate self and our true existence as pure consciousness.

The language of a dream is helpful because it points to the fact that everything we see is a perception without any solid reality behind it. The language of a dream is also problematic because it implies that there is a dreamer having the dream but, in non-dual realization, the whole of reality is seen to be a dream without a dreamer having it.

Look around you. I'm here in my favorite coffee shop. I'm seeing baristas and customers. I smell coffee and I see the bricks on the wall in front of me. Everything appears to exist. What if none of this is real in the way I've been trained to think of it? What if none of it has an existence independent of the experience of it?

If we have a non-dual awakening, we realize that the world and everything in it is a collection of experiences that we have assumed were connected to real things without any evidence that they were. If you think about, there's no reason for us to necessarily believe in a solid reality behind our experience. And this includes our experience of ourselves. All there is in reality, from our point of view, is a never-ending cascade of experiences and the existence of anything beyond those experiences is a matter of conjecture.

Imagine that you have a dream of a football game. In the dream, you are playing the game. In bed, you're lying there asleep. Where does the football field exist? In the room where you sleep there is no football field and there isn't one inside your head either. The football field of your dream has no material reality except in the dream. According to the non-dual tradition, our world and everything in it is a dream in pure consciousness. This may seem preposterous, but that's only because we've been taught otherwise.

If you are catapulted into an experience of non-dual oneness, you will never be the same again. A great deal of your experience may remain the same, but your confidence in the appearance of the world will be fundamentally undercut.

When you meet someone, you may talk to them as if they're separate from you, but when push comes to shove you know that the source of consciousness looking at you through their eyes is the same as the one looking at them through yours.

There are not two beings interacting. There is one consciousness that has created the experience of separation and the illusory experience of multiple entities perhaps so it could have the glorious experience of relating with another.

So, I would ask you to consider the question, what if there is no one having the experience you think you're having right now?

The belief that we are an entity that has experiences is one of the primary sources of our perceived separate existence. If you let go of this assumption, you just might tumble back into the indivisible wholeness of being.

Can you let go of your sense of self long enough to recognize that you are only consciousness and that is all there is?

CHAPTER TWENTY-EIGHT
THE SELF EVOLVES

The realization of *non-dual pure consciousness* as our true self brings about the end of the reign of the separate sense of self and also the beginning of a wider spiritual journey. Not our journey, but the journey of creation itself, as it realizes more and more of its manifest potentials through the further evolution of the sense of self that occurs in successive transformative leaps. As I see it, this creative endeavor is the whole purpose of spiritual life.

Our spiritual experiences, breakthroughs, openings, and energetic surges, are all stirrings of a new self that we are being invited to grow into. Our spiritual work reveals to us new possibilities in selfhood that can catalyze a shift out of our current sense of identity into something else that is trying to emerge through us. In this chapter, we will pull together many of the ideas we've explored so far and use them to define a three-stage process of evolving selfhood.

As I've come to understand it, this shift in identity occurs in three stages:

1. letting go of who we have been
2. discovering the possibilities of the emerging self
3. creatively expressing those new possibilities until that is who we are

Letting Go of Who We Have Been

We are a self – a somebody – or at least we think we are. We live inside an identity, a self-concept, a collection of ideas about the person we have been. That person has a name and a history. That person is good at some things and not good at others. He or she has fears, desires, memories, hopes, dreams, and aspirations.

The most valuable way to think about your sense of self is to think about it as a range of possibility. Some things are possible for the self that you are, other things are not. Spiritual growth is always an expansion of possibility.

In the first stage of evolving selfhood, we let go of the self that we think we are. There are many ways to do that, one of which is the practice of meditation that I have been explaining as The Practice of No Problem.

By learning to perfectly embrace the experience you are having in each and every moment, you generate inner spaciousness and ease of being. In this space, your attention begins to slip away from the habits of worry and self-concern that are the glue that hold your identity in place.

As your awareness is liberated from the sense that anything is wrong, you relax at physical, emotional, spiritual and ultimately existential levels of being. In this release, your awareness slips beyond the sphere of your familiar concerns and, eventually, beyond anything you've ever known. You find yourself more and more aware of a vast expanse of non-conceptual awareness beyond your ordinary mind.

As you acclimate to the experience of consciousness without understanding, you discover something wonderful. Here you are not a somebody. Here you don't know who you are. You experience the unimaginable freedom of awareness without identity. You are no longer tied to the solid sense of self that has always been your anchor and you enter into the unlimited possibility of who you really are.

This is the realm of spiritual realization that has been called Enlightenment, Satori, Illumination, God-Realization, Self-Actualization and many other lofty names. This depth of awakening frees us from the limitations of self-concept and self-concern and makes us available for a miraculous transformation of self.

Discovering the Possibilities of the Emerging Self

Initially, the freedom from the known that we experience is shocking but with more practice we become accustomed to it. And as we relax more deeply into the true depths of our being, we begin to notice something wonderful.

That incomprehensible expanse is not just emptiness. There are stirrings there, we are moved there. We feel things – delicate things, subtle things, amazing things. These are spiritual energies – energies of awakening – that abide out beyond what we know.

In the second stage of evolving selfhood, we allow ourselves to be moved by the subtle energetic currents that we discover emanating from the unknown. Learning to be moved in this way is a matter of learning to trust the inherent goodness of those energies.

The inner currents of spirit are there to move us, to guide us, to expand our being beyond the limitations of who we think we are into the fullness of what is possible. Being moved by these energies is not something we do, it is something we allow to happen.

At this stage of the process, you find yourself floating in an ocean of spiritual currents that want to carry you into expansive realms of being. All you have to do is learn to trust them enough to let go of anything that is inhibiting your growth.

As we experience the succession of insights, revelations, and awakenings that our practice brings, our confidence in the ultimate goodness of these spiritual currents of being will grow and we will find ourselves able to venture further and further out into new possibilities.

Expressing New Possibilities Until They Become Who We Are

As I said earlier, the most valuable way to think about self-identity is to think of it as a range of possibility. Very practically speaking, changing our sense of self is a matter of expanding the range of possibilities available to us.

The fruits of our spiritual practice invite a radical reconfiguration of what is possible not only for us, but for all human beings.

The transformation that we are exploring is not just about becoming a different human being. It is about becoming a different kind of human being. It is about letting go of our fundamental identity as a separate and isolated entity that lives in the midst of other separate and isolated entities. It is about discovering that there is nothing that

175

separates us. That we are One, even though our particularity and uniqueness are part of that Oneness.

As we begin to swirl together in the currents of a new way of being, we will find ourselves swept up into impossible possibilities. We will begin to feel things, see things and even know things that were simply not possible before. Together, we will learn to express these new possibilities, to give them a voice, to articulate them, to live them.

We will become what my colleague and friend Jeffrey Kripal calls "authors of the impossible."' We will bring a new way of being to life between us as we manifest in new ways.

CHAPTER TWENTY-NINE
THE FUTURE OF BEING HUMAN

My work, for many years, was exclusively focused on creating the conditions for collective awakening into what could be called Meta-Being. In this chapter, I want to explain that aspect of my work because it illustrates one profound possibility for the future of being human that could emerge as we embrace a new sense of self. I believe that spiritual liberation, and the freedom from the limits of our current sense of self, becomes most valuable when it is the foundation from which a new higher self can be born.

First of all, in relation to the term Meta-Being, I want to acknowledge that I came across the term first in the writings of the feminist theologian Mary Daly, who used it in opposition to the term New Being that had been coined by the theologian Paul Tillich. Daly preferred Meta-Being because it didn't imply a break with the past but rather a more encompassing form of being that included what came before. Similarly, I believe this sentiment of inclusivity is important.

I have already mentioned that for twenty years, I lived in an experimental spiritual community. During that time, all of the spiritual practice that we were doing was ultimately aimed at what we were calling collective or inter-subjective awakening. In the year 2001, I had the good fortune to be present for a particularly dramatic example of this kind of collective emergence and the best way for me to explain the phenomenon is simply to tell you what happened.

I was part of a small group of people on a two-month long retreat that included focused discussions every evening. It was in these discussions that something profound started to be expressed by some of the members of the group.

During one of these meetings, I experienced a shift in identity that has had a defining influence on my life and work ever since. At one point in the meeting, I felt deeply inspired to speak and started to think about what I would say. Then I stopped and, rather than formulate my words beforehand, I simply allowed them to rise up and pass through my mouth.

I found myself speaking words before I knew what I was saying. It felt like something was speaking through me and describing my experience from a vantage point I had never had before and with more precision than I ever could. On the one hand, it felt like I wasn't speaking at all, and yet the words being spoken were more mine than any I'd ever spoken before. The evening meetings continued and more and more of us entered into this mysterious space of engaged surrender.

Once everyone in the group had entered into this shared awakening, a wild energy swirled through us and everyone was speaking with a profound clarity, conviction, and sensitivity beyond anything they had known before. We all seemed to have access to what I might now call Meta-Being – a source of wisdom that encompassed all of us and gave us access to possibilities beyond our imagination.

It was not just that each individual was speaking from the pure consciousness of non-dual awareness. It was as if the group of us had become fused into a higher being and that higher being was speaking through each of us. It was like sharing a single mind with everyone in the room. I had never dreamed of anything like it before.

From that time forward, I've dedicated myself to discovering how to create the conditions that allow this Meta-Being to be awakened and sustained between people. Not just in focused discussions on retreat, but as the ongoing background of life. Right now, we live within the shared assumption that we are separate individuals with independent consciousness. That is the background that shapes human life. What I experienced was the possibility that we live in a world in which we all know that we are One and we see the One acting in unique ways through every seemingly separate individual.

One of the things that I've learned about the process of collective emergence is that it depends on our willingness to liberate ourselves from our current sense of identity so that we are available for something more. We have all learned to think of ourselves as an isolated entity – a separate thing in a universe filled with other things. Unless we see through the assumption of independent existence to a significant degree, a new form of self cannot be born.

As we let go of the false beliefs and assumptions that hold our current identity of separation and isolation in place, we discover that the person we think we are is nothing more than a collection of stories about ourselves. Underneath all those stories, there is no 'me' that is not just another story about 'me.' There is no solid self that exists independent of our ideas about it.

This is the great realization of emptiness that is talked about in many of the world's great spiritual traditions. It shows us that our current sense of self is not immutable – it can change. We can grow into a different sense of self – not just the same self with better qualities, but something dramatically different. We can become a different kind of human.

As we move further and further away from the stories about us and deeper and deeper into the direct experience of being, we enter into a profoundly free and fluid state of awareness. From here, we can discover together how to expand into a sense of self bigger than we ever imagined and at the same time find our True Self.

One possible future for humanity is what I experienced as the collective awakening of Meta-Being. I am sure there are an infinite field of possible human futures. Whether Meta-Being is our future or not, there is no way to know, but experiencing the miracle of this dramatically different sense of self left me utterly convinced that what we are is not an immutable fixed entity.

We are a fluid flow of conscious energy that has gotten temporarily frozen in the dream of our current sense of self. Spiritual liberation means liberating the flow of conscious energy so that it can find new shapes of self to occupy and explore new potentials in perception to manifest.

If we let go of who we think we are, the energetic flow that we are will be free to move into whatever is next, and next after that, and next after that. This is the divine journey of discovery that the universe will resume as soon as we are done holding on to who we are.

CHAPTER THIRTY
LOVE, HEALING AND THE
JOURNEY HOME

I believe that spiritual growth under the right conditions is as natural as breathing. And I believe the conditions of our world are the perfect conditions for spiritual growth. The person you are right now, with all of your challenges and strengths, pain and joys, failures and victories, is exactly the perfect person for the journey ahead. And your life, exactly as it is, is offering you the exact conditions to stimulate growth.

In this final chapter, I will share why I believe that existence is an unending emergence of pure love - a perfect and continuous homecoming, in spite of and in a sense because of, all the tragedy, pain and the unnecessary suffering that is endured by so many of us. I would start by asserting that the degree to which we recognize that suffering is unnecessary is evidence that, somewhere, we already know that love is the ground of existence.

This universe was born out of love and our desire for spiritual fulfillment is an expression of that love, an extension of that love, and the fulfillment of that love. Human life is challenging. We find ourselves caught in the middle between the reality of Love and the reality of suffering.

What is Love? Love is what we feel when we recognize something that is worth devoting our life to. The things we love are the things that make life worth living. They allow us to feel at home in the world and relax deeply and completely into the experience of being.

We wake up in a world that often feels harsh and alien to us. It is unpredictable and beyond our control. We experience pain and suffering and we learn to protect ourselves from the perceived dangers that surround us. Some of us experience tremendous hardship, others have a relatively easier time, but no one is completely unscathed by the challenges of existence. We are all wounded and in need of healing.

Because we have been hurt, we conclude at a deep and unconscious level that we do not belong here. The beginning of our spiritual search is often an attempt to escape and discover some place where we truly belong.

We imagine that we are lost and we feel compelled to find our way home. We have fallen out of love and long to rediscover the love that we know is our true home.

Our early seeking is a series of attempts, often meandering and haphazard, to find our way home. We try practices, workshops, methods, communities, and teachers. Each time we wonder if this is it. Is this where I belong? Is this my home?

Spiritual awakening is the ultimate homecoming. It is the discovery of a home that you can never leave and the realization that you have never been anywhere but home all along. This human life – with all of its hardships and joys, victories and defeats, pains and pleasures – is home. We are already home. This is it and always has been.

The experience of life has left us with inner wounds of separation – habits of retraction, recoil, and isolation, that leave us trapped in a severely limited sense of self. Somewhere deep inside, we always knew that this sense of limitation was unreal and we longed to find our way back to reality.

Periodically along the way, we had moments of profound mystical opening and our awareness was temporarily released from the distortion of contraction. In these moments, we suddenly and unexpectedly found ourselves home in a place so perfect that we had no desire to be anywhere else. We were home in the most profound way imaginable. When these miraculous episodes inevitably left us, we found ourselves back in our limited and contracted self.

If we are not careful at these moments, we will mistakenly reassert the illusion of being lost. Because the experience of contraction has returned, we are tempted to assume that we are no longer home. In our alarm, we may embark on a quest to recapture what we imagine we have lost. We restart our spiritual quest, forgetting that we have already discovered that this is it. If, on the other hand, we have the fortitude to remember that we have already arrived, the true spiritual journey can begin.

The true spiritual journey is not the journey that takes us home. In fact, it is not our journey at all. It is the expansion of the only true home there is – consciousness. The true journey is the evolution of consciousness.

The fact that consciousness evolves does not mean that we have not already arrived. Consciousness is never less than complete. It is always a full expression of the experience that is currently available to be had, even though it is also not the limit of what is possible.

Can we hold our current reality as perfect at the same time that we recognize that it will inevitably grow into more? Can we live in a total fullness that is destined to be more full? The spiritual life requires us to embrace an unconditional wholeness that relentlessly continues to grow.

The experience of being someone who experiences the contraction of past pain and suffering, who has occasional moments of release and relief, and may even experience periodic illuminations of spirit, is the human experience. It is whole and complete, beautiful and miraculous, exactly as it is. Life is in need of nothing more. At the same time, we are invited to a journey of ascension in which the human experience will expand beyond its current form into the unknown wholeness of tomorrow, and perhaps ultimately even beyond the experience of being human.

Initially, our spiritual practice is taken up in service of our personal journey home. When we discover that we were always already home, a new journey begins that places our practice at the service of something much bigger than our limited selves.

We might do a sitting practice like meditation, or chanting, or singing, or a movement practice like dance or yoga. The form our practice takes is not as important as what the practice is in service of. In order for our energy to be available for the larger journey, our practice must be anchored in an unshakeable conviction that we are already home - whole and complete.

Spiritual practice becomes potent once we are convinced that there is nowhere to go other than here. Only then are we able to unconditionally let go. When we deeply relax all of our conscious and unconscious attempts to get somewhere else, to protect ourselves and to manipulate the world, something glorious happens. The contractions that have accumulated over a lifetime naturally and effortlessly begin to release.

We will feel this physically, emotionally, and cognitively. We might feel pain in our body as tightness dissolves and passes away. We may go through emotional upheavals of joy, sorrow, fear, or bliss, as emotions that have been repressed bubble to the surface. And as our minds become free of limiting beliefs, we will experience profound insight that will reveal the secrets of the universe.

We do not need to control this journey. The only effort we need to make is whatever it takes to remember that we are already home, and resist the temptation to try to control the unfolding that has begun. We will be guided through physical healings, emotional releases, and mystical revelations in exactly the form that is required for our growth.

As we allow the larger spiritual journey to unfold, it will become clear that the effort we made to find our way home was what got us to the starting point of the true spiritual odyssey. It is like walking from the back car of a train to the front car only to realize that the real journey is the happening along the tracks outside the train. We are not on an individual journey, the entire human race is on a journey, and ultimately consciousness itself is evolving.

Our personal journey ends when we realize that we are already home.

Then we have the opportunity to participate in the magnificent journey of conscious evolution. The contractions that release in our being are not just ours, they are contractions in consciousness itself, and as we all release the binds that tie us new possibilities for life reveal themselves.

We then have the opportunity to live into these possibilities and recreate the world.

As we learn to allow the larger journey of spirit to unfold through us, we discover what we are here for. We are not here to suffer and contract. We are the medium within which a natural process of growth takes place. That process will release constraints and unleash our true potential as part of the larger liberation of consciousness.

We have no way to imagine where the larger journey of consciousness will take us, but that journey of existence is our journey nonetheless.

When we let go of any attempt to be anywhere other than here, all of our energy is available to do the invisible work of conscious evolution. This is an endeavor worthy of devoting our life to. This is the journey we were born for.

Can you imagine any Love greater than this?

ABOUT THE AUTHOR

Jeff Carreira is a meditation teacher, mystical philosopher and author who teaches tirelessly to a growing number of people throughout the world.

As a teacher, Jeff offers retreats and courses guiding individuals in a form of meditation called The Practice of No Problem. Through this simple and effective meditation technique, Jeff has led thousands of people in the journey beyond the confines of fear and self-concern into the expansive liberated awareness that is our true home.

Ultimately, Jeff is interested in defining a new way of being in the world that will move us from our current paradigm of separation and isolation into an emerging paradigm of unity and wholeness. He is exploring some of the most revolutionary ideas and systems of thought in the domains of spirituality, consciousness, and human development. He teaches people how to question their own experience so deeply that previously held assumptions about the nature of reality fall away to create space for dramatic shifts in understanding.

Jeff is passionate about philosophy because he is passionate about the power of ideas to shape how we perceive reality and how we live together. His enthusiasm for learning is infectious, and he enjoys addressing student groups and inspiring them to develop their own powers of inquiry. He has taught students at colleges and universities throughout the world.

Jeff is the author of numerous books including: *The Miracle of Meditation*, *The Practice of No Problem*, *Embrace All That You Are*, *Philosophy Is Not a Luxury*, *Radical Inclusivity*, *The Soul of a New Self*, and *Paradigm Shifting*. For more information about Jeff or to book him for a speaking engagement, visit: www.jeffcarreira.com

Made in the USA
Middletown, DE
09 June 2019